ONE POT
ONE PORTION

For my Momma, Anna, Henry, and for my Dad.

It's always better when we're together.

ONE POT
ONE PORTION

SIMPLE SPEEDY RECIPES JUST FOR <u>YOU</u>

Eleanor
Wilkinson

EBURY
PRESS

Introduction   6

COMFORT   14

FRESH   56

SIMPLE   96

SPECIAL   136

SWEET   176

Ingredient Index   218

Acknowledgements   223

One Pot One Portion is the book for people who cook, eat, or live alone and are tired of washing-up.

In a culinary world that caters for families, couples, or large gatherings, we seem to have overlooked the solo cook. With recipes almost always for four or more, those of us who cook for just ourselves must either fill our freezers, feed our friends or be forced to endure reheated spag bol for the next three days. Don't get me wrong, batch cooking can be a great, resourceful way of preparing food but, no matter how much you love shepherd's pie, it's hard to find joy in the monotony of eating from the same Pyrex dish every night, and this is only amplified when you're the only one eating. Not to mention, if you're cooking for yourself, you're also always on clean-up duty. This is where One Pot, One Portion comes in.

But where did it all start? Not too long ago I quit my job to pursue a career in food, my long-term relationship ended, and I began living by myself. The simultaneous occurrence of these three events meant that, despite cooking being my biggest and most long-lasting passion, I found myself not wanting to cook for myself due, in part, to tiresome and unappetising leftovers and the seemingly endless mountains of washing-up. I realised that one-portion recipes weren't enough, they had to be one-pot too. As bread is to butter, or crumble is to custard, One Pot is to One Portion: they make sense together.

Though I created the series for myself initially, I started sharing the recipes online too. The response was truly overwhelming, and showed me just how many people out there are in the same predicament, and that we all want to eat well!

So, whether you live alone or simply find yourself cooking for one from time to time, this book is from me to you. Though you might end up making these recipes for loved ones, primarily I have written this for you. From one solo cook to another, I truly hope you find something in this book that encourages you to spend time on yourself, and for yourself, making a meal that will bring you joy.

FOOD AS SELF-CARE

From single 20-somethings, to families feeding toddlers, to parents whose children have flown the nest, and those who find themselves spending more time alone as they get older, it seems that many of us are looking for little ways to take extra good care of ourselves and that's exactly what I want to encourage you to do. I want to make cooking a joyous act of self-care.

Food is love, but while it can be easy to show that love to others, taking the time to feed yourself can feel overwhelming and unnecessary. Even for someone who loves both food and cooking as much as I do, the prospect can feel like a chore. I want to make cooking for yourself – both the process and the result – easy, enjoyable and delicious. I want to bridge the gap between ease and excitement, ensuring variety without additional effort.

I know first-hand the slight dread that can come at the end of a long day, just when you think all work is done, when you realise you still need to make dinner for yourself. As I mentioned earlier, I created this concept and hence this book for myself, and I hope that these recipes can provide some relief from that dread, and perhaps even allow you to look forward to cooking for yourself.

I completely understand that part of the joy of food comes from sharing it and, in my opinion, sharing food is one of the ultimate forms of love. But I want this book to encourage you to spend that time, energy and love on yourself. Because you deserve it. Because there is so much joy to be found in doing something just for you. When there is no one else to consider, you can revel in the luxury of selfish choice, prioritising your wants and needs, and allowing your food to fit into your life in the way you need it to in that moment – whether that's a quick dish that takes little time on a busy day, or a comforting meal on a day when you need a moment of warm calm. So, I hope you revel in this book, its recipes and the reminder that caring for yourself is important and necessary and that food can be a part of that care.

ABOUT ME

Since I was old enough to hold a spoon, food has been my greatest passion and my main joy in life. Over the years, I have documented my life through food, writing holiday diaries memorialising not what we did or where we went, but what we ate. Now, I've turned that documentation into a job, creating and sharing recipes with others.

Food is my fiction, transporting me to another place, even if just for a moment, and some of my earliest memories relate to food and cooking. My parents travelled a lot, both with us and before us, so, although I grew up in rural East Yorkshire, our family meals often took inspiration from other cuisines. Dinners we thought were staples in all households were, in fact, entirely made-up. There has been more than one occasion over the years when I discovered a food that I thought was real, was really a cunning ploy to make us eat something we were convinced we didn't like. (Did I think bubble-gum tuna was a real thing until I was 16? Yes. What was it really? Salmon.)

For me, food is the epitome of finding excitement and joy in the everyday. That excitement is what gets me out of bed in the morning and is what I want to share with others. I have spent many hours poring over cookbooks, reading them from cover to cover, searching for inspiration and developing my own recipes and takes on classic meals. It's a huge privilege to share my own creations with others online and now, in this book.

My entire food ethos revolves around 'good food'. What 'good food' looks like is different from day to day and meal to meal but, in essence, to me all food is good food. Sometimes it's an elaborate dinner that takes several hours and many ingredients to make. At other times, it's a piece of soft white bread (the cheaper the better) with an illegal, but entirely necessary, amount of butter. I also believe that food and mood go hand in hand. How we feel has the potential to affect how we eat, and I think that's wonderful. How lovely that on days where we're in need of comfort, we can find solace in a warming bowl of pasta. How fun that, when life gives us opportunities to celebrate, we can share food and create memories with loved ones. While food often uplifts and changes your mood for the better, I also think it's amazing that food can let you sit with your feelings, whatever they may be. This is especially pertinent when cooking for one – and the personalisation and power of food is a theme that runs through everything I do, especially in this book.

HOW TO USE THIS BOOK

This book isn't fussy, it doesn't overcomplicate things. I don't think you need to have fancy ingredients or complex concepts in order to enjoy a really great meal. And that's what I want to give you from this book, a really darn great meal.

As I have said, one of the joys of cooking for one is the freedom of choice that means you get to decide what you eat and when you eat it, so I actively chose not to divide this book up by meal types. I don't want to limit you to only eating breakfast foods at breakfast, or puddings after your evening meal. Where's the fun in that! You want lasagne for breakfast? I'm certainly not going to be the one to stop you. Despite what years of diet culture may have tried to convince us of, eating is entirely personal, individual and unique to everyone.

I want you to take a moment to check in with yourself, to think about how you're feeling, what you need on that day or in that moment, and how your food can help with that. As such, I have divided this book not by meal type or by cooking times, but by feeling. Ask yourself what you fancy eating that day, then flick through the chapter that most aligns with that feeling and find a recipe that brings you what you need, whether that be warmth, energy, more time, peace or joy.

1. **COMFORT**: Recipes to bring you ultimate warmth, for days when you need to feel cosy and homely.

2. **FRESH**: Food packed with colour and vibrancy, for times when you want your food to energise you and bring a little zing to your day.

3. **SIMPLE**: For when you have enough on your plate and you'd like your food to require little time or fresh ingredients. Satisfaction without stress.

4. **SPECIAL**: When you want to show yourself a little extra love. Recipes that take more time or money but bring another level of joy.

5. **SWEET**: For when you need extra sweetness in your day, food that is impossible not to enjoy, and not just for dessert.

Hopefully, across the chapters in this book, you'll find everything you need to fulfil all requirements. So have fun, eat well, and enjoy it as much as possible.

RECIPE PAIRINGS AND AVOIDING FOOD WASTE

We've solved the dilemma of cooking for one without the consequences of a sink full of washing-up, but that's not enough if you're left puzzling over what to do with half a butternut squash that may or may not have been in the fridge for several weeks. So, for every recipe in this book, I have provided a partner recipe that uses one or more of the same fresh ingredients. Leftover beef mince after making Hash Brown Cottage Pie? Why not try my Smash Burger Flatbread? Used an egg white to make Crispy Chilli Beef Noodles? Why not make Lemon Bread and Butter Pudding with the yolk? You'll find the suggested pairing at the bottom of every recipe.

Then, at the end of this book, I have provided an ingredient index (see page 218) so, if you don't fancy the suggestion on the recipe page, take a peek at the index and see if there's anything else you like the sound of. You can use this to plan your meals ahead of time if needed, or for spontaneous inspiration, with the added bonus of fighting food waste and ensuring you get the most from your ingredients, and your money.

COOKING FOR ONE

You'll have gathered by now that simplicity is my aim with this book – these recipes are here to make your life easier, not more complicated. So don't worry, I'm not going to suggest you run out and buy lots of specialist equipment. However, if the One Pot, One Portion life is for you, there are a few things that will make things even easier.

EQUIPMENT: SCALES

Due to their nature, single portions require slightly more accuracy when it comes to measuring ingredients as there's less room for error. I highly recommend using digital scales as opposed to analogue scales or measuring cups. When working in 5 gram increments, that accuracy can make a difference. Plus, it can save you washing-up. I find that the easiest ways to measure ingredients where possible are:

A. To place your pot or pan directly on the scales and weigh straight into it, as opposed to weighing into other bowls. Also note, 1ml of water = 1g.

B. Let's say you're measuring pasta – set the bag of pasta on the scales and reset it back to 0g. When you take pasta out of the bag and put it into the pan, the scales will go into minus numbers and you can use this to work out how much pasta you have taken out (-80g on the scales means you have 80g in the pan).

Occasionally a recipe may use an additional bowl or jug, though I have tried only to do this when truly necessary. If possible, I try and use the bowl that I'm going to end up eating out of.

EQUIPMENT: POTS, PANS AND SKILLETS

There are a variety of recipes in this book. Some only require a pan on the hob. Others are cooked on a roasting tray in the oven. Then there are a few that require an individual-sized dish that can work both on a hob and in the oven. There are several options you can go for here. Primarily, you want to avoid anything with a handle that isn't made of metal, and choose a pan that is oven-safe up to at least 230°C.

My preference is for a small cast-iron skillet which you can find online for around £15. I have a couple, ranging from 6.5–8 inches (17–20cm) in diameter and they're perfect for one-portion cooking – suitable for any hob, including induction, and perfectly safe for the oven. Cast iron has a reputation for being high-maintenance, but the more you use it, the easier and the better it gets. Stainless steel pans are also an excellent option, and both stainless steel and cast iron should last an eternity if correctly looked after. I would also recommend a small pie dish, approximately 7–8 inches (18–20cm) in length. These are perfect, not only for pies, but also for sticky toffee pudding, brownies and crumbles.

This chapter is for days when you need your food to bring warmth and solace. Hot bowls filled with decadent dishes to soothe the mind, the body and the soul, best eaten on the sofa under a warm blanket. Here you'll find family favourites such as toad in the hole, fish pie and chilli con carne con rice, alongside new takes on comforting classics, such as crispy chilli beef noodles, risotto carbonara and chicken and broccoli alfredo.

COMFORT

SAUSAGE, FENNEL + CHILLI PASTA

Prep Time: 10 minutes
Cook Time: 25 minutes

Savoury sausage, fresh fennel and hot chilli are a match made in heaven and the rich heat in this dish makes it the perfect winter warmer. The fennel flavour is subtle, so I'd recommend this even for those with a slight aniseed aversion. Cooking the pasta in the same pot as all the other ingredients, as we do here, means all the starches stick around and combine with the pecorino to create the silkiest sauce to coat the pasta. A warming bowl of cosy comfort.

1 tsp extra virgin olive oil

2 pork sausages

2 garlic cloves, thinly sliced
  into strips

85g fennel bulb, thinly sliced
  into strips

300ml water

½ chicken or vegetable stock pot

85g short pasta (e.g. rigatoni
  or penne)

30g pecorino, grated, plus extra for
  serving

salt and black pepper

To serve:

½–1 red chilli, finely chopped

Heat the oil in a saucepan over a medium-high heat. Remove the skin from the sausages and break the meat into pieces using your hands, then add to the hot oil. Fry for 4–5 minutes until golden brown. Then add in the garlic and fennel and cook for 3 more minutes.

Add in the water, stock pot and pasta, mix everything together and turn the heat down slightly so the stock is gently boiling (don't put a lid on). Cook for 15 minutes, stirring occasionally to ensure it cooks evenly. Depending on the size of your pan, you may need to add a splash more water, but you want most of it to be absorbed by the time the pasta has cooked, so be sparing.

Most of the liquid should be absorbed now, so add the grated pecorino and mix to emulsify with the remaining liquid. Season with pepper; taste, and add salt as necessary (the cheese, stock and sausage are all salty, so make sure to taste first).

Plate up and finish with finely chopped fresh chilli and another sprinkling of pecorino.

USE YOUR LEFTOVER ...

sausages:
page 120

CHICKEN PARMY

Prep Time: 15 minutes
Cook Time: 45 minutes

I was first introduced to chicken Parmy by my Australian friends at cookery school. A pub classic over there (and different from the chicken Parmo that you would find in North-East England), here I've reimagined it slightly so it can be made in one pot. Chicken breast layered with thick ham, a generous scatter of cheese and a crisp coating of breadcrumbs, all nestled in a deep tomato sauce – this is heavenly. It's fairly rich, so I suggest serving it with a crisp green side salad.

2 tsp extra virgin olive oil
½ red onion, finely diced
2 garlic cloves, finely chopped
1 tbsp tomato purée
150g tinned tomatoes
75ml water
10g fresh basil leaves, finely
    chopped, a few reserved
    for garnish
1 chicken breast
1 slice of thick-cut ham
    (preferably smoked)
60g mozzarella, grated (or torn,
    if using fresh)
15g Parmesan, grated
20g breadcrumbs
salt and black pepper

To serve:
your favourite side salad

Preheat the oven to 200°C (180°C fan).

Heat the oil in a small ovenproof frying pan or baking dish over a medium heat. Add the onion and fry for 5 minutes until golden and soft. Then add the garlic along with the tomato purée and cook for 3 more minutes.

Tip in the tinned tomatoes, water and chopped basil. Mix everything together, season with salt and pepper, then take the pan/dish off the heat.

Put your chicken breast on top of the sauce and season again with salt and pepper. Place the ham on top of the chicken, then scatter the mozzarella over the top of the ham. Sprinkle the Parmesan over the mozzarella, and, finally, sprinkle the breadcrumbs on top. Place in the oven and bake for 35 minutes or until the chicken has fully cooked through and the topping is golden and crisp.

Top with the reserved basil leaves and serve with a salad.

NOTE: If you want to make this vegetarian, substitute the chicken for half a large aubergine, scored across the flesh, and leave out the ham. Bake for the same amount of time.

USE YOUR LEFTOVER...
chicken breast:
page 89

CRISPY CHILLI BEEF NOODLES

Crispy chilli beef is a truly wonderful thing, and this version is slightly fresher than the classic takeaway, while still providing the same comfort. As with many recipes in this book, you can switch up the vegetables depending on your preferences, or what you have in, and the stir-fry sauce is made from store-cupboard staples. This is also a great recipe to use up any leftover egg whites, but if you're cracking an egg specially, check out page 219 for other ideas on how to use up the leftover egg yolk.

Prep Time: 20 minutes
Cook Time: 10 minutes

Whisk the egg white in a bowl with a fork to break it up. Add the steak to the egg white and coat evenly. Add the cornflour and a pinch of salt to the steak and egg mixture and mix again. The steak should be covered in a thick, gloopy coating.

In a large frying pan or wok, heat the vegetable oil over a high heat. Let the oil get really hot, then add in the steak, spreading it out into one layer to make sure it gets nice and brown and crispy. Fry for around 4 minutes, turning halfway through cooking.

Once the steak is golden and crisp on all sides, add in the onion, pepper, chilli(es) and garlic and stir-fry for 2 more minutes. Finally, add in the noodles and all of the sauce ingredients and toss everything together. Cook for a final minute until the noodles are soft and the sauce is thick, glossy and coats everything evenly. Finish with the spring onions, tossing them through just before serving.

USE YOUR LEFTOVER...
egg yolk:
page 38

For the beef:
1 egg white
1 sirloin steak, sliced into 1cm strips, cut across the grain
1½ tbsp cornflour
pinch of salt

For the stir fry:
1½ tbsp vegetable oil
½ white onion, finely sliced into strips
½ red pepper, finely sliced into strips
1–2 red chillies (depending on your preference and how hot the chillies are), finely sliced into strips
1 garlic clove, grated or finely chopped
1 pack of medium straight-to-wok noodles
2 spring onions, finely sliced

For the sauce:
1 tbsp soy sauce
1 tbsp ketchup
2 tsp rice wine vinegar
1 tsp brown sugar
2 tbsp water

CHICKEN + BROCCOLI ALFREDO

Prep Time: 5 minutes
Cook Time: 10 minutes

There aren't many things more comforting than a creamy pasta dish, but what I love about this alfredo is that it has a certain lightness to it that, in essence, means you can eat loads of it. And who doesn't want that? Using fresh pasta is handy when making one-pot pasta dishes, as it's quicker to cook and doesn't require as much liquid. Once you've tried this, you'll be making it on repeat, so change up the pasta shape to keep things interesting and just modify the water quantity as necessary.

1 tsp extra virgin olive oil
1 chicken breast, cut into thin strips
70g broccoli, cut into small florets
2 garlic cloves, finely chopped
½ tsp paprika
½ tsp dried mixed herbs
90g fresh penne or other short pasta
125ml water
½ chicken stock pot
3 tbsp double cream
25g Parmesan, grated
small handful (5g) of finely
   chopped fresh parsley
black pepper

To serve:
bread, to mop up the sauce

Heat the oil in a saucepan over a medium heat. Once hot, add in the chicken, broccoli, garlic, paprika and mixed herbs and season with pepper. Sauté for 4–5 minutes until the chicken has some colour but isn't cooked all the way through.

Add in the pasta, water, stock pot, cream and Parmesan. Give it a good stir and let it simmer for 4–5 minutes until the pasta and the chicken are cooked and the sauce has thickened slightly.

Add in the fresh parsley and stir through before serving. Mop up any extra sauce with a piece of bread.

USE YOUR LEFTOVER ...

chicken breast:
page 64

MATAR PANEER

Prep Time: 10 minutes
Cook Time: 30 minutes

Paneer never fails to bring me joy. I adore its slight rubberiness, its resistance, its squeaky chew. Such power from such a humble cheese. Here it's cooked in a rich, spiced sauce balanced with little bursts of fresh peas. It's just calling to be scooped up with handfuls of soft, buttery flatbread in front of your favourite tv show.

2 tbsp ghee (or 1 tbsp butter
   and 1 tbsp vegetable oil)
½ white onion, finely chopped
120g paneer, diced
2 garlic cloves, grated
   or finely chopped
10g fresh ginger, grated
   or finely chopped
2 cardamom pods, lightly crushed
½ cinnamon stick
¼ tsp ground coriander
¼ tsp ground cumin
¼ tsp ground turmeric
150g passata
150ml water
5–10g fresh coriander,
   finely chopped
½ tsp garam masala
75g frozen peas
1 tbsp double cream
1 green chilli (optional),
   finely chopped
salt

To serve:
naan, paratha or flatbread

Heat the ghee (or butter and oil) in a frying pan over a medium-high heat and, once melted, add in the onion and the paneer. Let these fry for 10 minutes, stirring frequently. You want the onion to be golden but not brown, so keep an eye on it and turn the heat down if necessary.

Once the onion is done, add in the garlic, ginger, cardamom, cinnamon, ground coriander, cumin and turmeric and cook for 3–4 minutes until the spices smell fragrant. Add in the passata and water and let them simmer for another 10 minutes.

Once the mix has reduced slightly, add in most of the fresh coriander, saving a little for the top, along with the garam masala, peas, cream and chilli, if using, and simmer for a final 3–4 minutes or until the peas are cooked. Taste and season with salt.

Serve up and sprinkle over the rest of the fresh coriander. Eat with your favourite bread.

USE YOUR LEFTOVER ...

paneer:
page 148

LASAGNE

Prep Time: 5 minutes
Cook Time: 45 minutes

I feel as though I shouldn't really have favourite recipes in this book as they are all very dear to me, but this lasagne holds a special place in my heart. Just don't mention it in Italy, ok? A traditionally time-consuming, somewhat strenuous dish that leaves a mountain of washing-up, this version, though not traditional, fully replicates the flavours and feel of a layered lasagne in a simple, stress-free way. I hope you enjoy it as much as I do.

extra virgin olive oil
½ white onion, finely diced
2 garlic cloves, finely diced or grated
1 tbsp tomato purée
125g beef mince (you could also
   use a vegetarian mince)
200g tinned tomatoes
½ beef stock pot
100ml water
½ tsp dried mixed herbs
75g fresh lasagne sheets
60g mascarpone
60g mozzarella, grated
salt and black pepper

Add a little olive oil to a small ovenproof frying pan or baking dish on a medium heat and fry off the onion for around 5 minutes until softened and golden. Add in the garlic and cook for another 2–3 minutes.

Squeeze in the tomato purée and cook for 2 minutes before adding in the beef mince and cooking until browned.

Add in the tinned tomatoes, stock pot, water and mixed herbs. Let this simmer and reduce for around 15 minutes over a low heat. While this is cooking, preheat the grill to 200°C.

Cut the fresh lasagne sheets into quarters. Once the sauce is rich and reduced, taste and season well with salt and pepper, then mix in the lasagne sheets and cook for 3–4 minutes with the lid off until they are cooked but still al dente. Take off the heat and spoon dollops of mascarpone on top, then cover with the grated mozzarella. Grill for 10–15 minutes until golden and bubbling.

USE YOUR LEFTOVER...
beef mince:
page 42

PUMPKIN CURRY

I was lucky enough to spend two summers in Fiji while I was at university, volunteering with an educational charity and living with two families who are among the most generous, warm-hearted people I have ever met. I like to think I have a 'foodographic' memory, so whilst I may not always remember what I did, or where I went, I will always remember the food I ate – this pumpkin curry takes me straight back to the villages in Fiji. Don't skip past this recipe; it may not be a looker, but it really is delicious.

Prep Time: 10 minutes
Cook Time: 40 minutes

Heat the olive oil in a pan over a medium heat. Add the onion and cook for 5 minutes or so, until softened and starting to colour. Add the garlic and cook for a couple of minutes before adding the cumin seeds, mustard seeds, fenugreek seeds and curry powder. Cook for 2–3 minutes until fragrant.

Add in the butternut squash, water and stock pot. Put a lid on the pan and bring to the boil before turning down the heat and simmering for 30 minutes.

After 30 minutes, take the lid off. The butternut squash will be tender, so crush most of it with a fork, leaving some chunkier bits. Simmer for another couple of minutes to thicken the sauce slightly.

Top with green chilli, if using, and serve with roti.

1½ tbsp extra virgin olive oil
½ white onion, finely diced
2 garlic cloves, grated
  or finely chopped
½ tsp cumin seeds
½ tsp mustard seeds
½ tsp fenugreek seeds (also called
  methi seeds)
¼ tsp curry powder
150g butternut squash, peeled and
  cut into 2.5cm cubes
300ml water
½ vegetable stock pot

To serve:
green chilli, finely sliced (optional)
roti

USE YOUR LEFTOVER:
butternut squash: page 32

FISH PIE

Prep Time: 10 minutes
Cook Time: 35 minutes

As a family classic, making fish pie for one feels sort of excessive, not to mention exhausting. I'm sure you'll agree that there's something about making mashed potato for one that just isn't appealing. This fish pie couldn't be easier, though, as I've switched out the mashed potato for thin slices of potato that simultaneously soften down and crisp up in the oven. You can use a fish pie mix for this, or just one fish fillet. If opting for the former, a frozen mix is a useful way to avoid waste. If opting for the latter, I would choose salmon as it holds its shape so it doesn't overcook as it bakes.

15g butter
1 tbsp plain flour
175ml milk
2 tbsp crème fraîche
125g skinless fish fillet, cut into
  2.5cm cubes – use a fish pie mix
  or a mixture of your favourite fish
1 tsp finely chopped fresh parsley,
  plus extra to garnish
1 tsp finely chopped fresh dill, plus
  extra to garnish
30g frozen peas
1 medium potato (150–175g),
  cut into ½cm slices
30g Cheddar, grated
salt and black pepper

Preheat the oven to 220°C (200°C fan).

Start by making the white sauce. Place an ovenproof frying pan or baking dish over a medium heat, and melt in the butter. Once melted, stir in the flour and let that cook off for 2 minutes before slowly stirring in the milk until you have a smooth sauce.

Turn off the heat and add in the crème fraîche, fish, herbs and peas and mix thoroughly. Season with salt and pepper.

Lay the potato slices in concentric circles on top of the fish mixture. Season with salt, then scatter the grated cheese over the top.

Bake in the oven for 30 minutes or until the potatoes are soft and golden brown on top. Let it cool slightly and finish with a final sprinkle of herbs before eating.

USE YOUR LEFTOVER

crème fraîche:
page 191

CREAMY BAKED GNOCCHI WITH SQUASH + SAUSAGE

Prep Time: 10 minutes
Cook Time: 60 minutes

Roasting gnocchi, as opposed to boiling it, changes its character completely, turning it from soft and pillowy, to crisp and bouncy. Crispy sausage pieces and sweet squash mingle together and, if you chop everything to a similar size as the gnocchi, you can just about get a piece of everything in every bite. You can easily substitute the sausages, cream cheese and milk with plant-based alternatives to make this vegan, too, as I have done on occasion.

200g butternut squash, peeled and cut into 2.5cm cubes

150g cherry tomatoes, cut in half

1 tsp dried sage, or 7–8 fresh sage leaves

½ tsp dried thyme, or 3–4 fresh thyme sprigs

extra virgin olive oil

2 garlic cloves, finely chopped

125g gnocchi

2–3 sausages (meat or vegetarian)

2 tbsp cream cheese

3 tbsp milk

salt and black pepper

Preheat the oven to 200°C (180°C fan).

Put the squash and tomatoes in an ovenproof baking dish (bigger is better to help things get a little crispier), with the dried herbs (if using fresh herbs, don't add them yet), a good drizzle of olive oil and some salt and pepper. Roast for 30 minutes until soft.

Add the garlic to the pan along with the gnocchi. Break the sausages into small pieces (if using meat sausages, you may want to remove the casing first). Drizzle with a little more olive oil for extra crispness and roast for another 30 minutes. If using fresh herbs, scatter them over for the final 10 minutes with a little extra oil.

Once baked, add in the cream cheese and the milk. Give it a good stir until creamy and delicious. Add more milk to loosen if needed before serving.

USE YOUR LEFTOVER butternut squash: page 40

PEANUT CURRY WITH TOFU + POTATOES

Prep Time: 10 minutes
Cook Time: 25 minutes

This recipe takes inspiration from a Thai Massaman curry, which will almost always be my choice if I see it on a menu. Cardamom is perhaps my favourite of all the spices and its slightly floral sweetness is perfect with a rich coconut sauce, creamy peanut butter and zesty lime. If you haven't tried tofu puffs before, then you're in for a treat – even if you think you dislike tofu, I really encourage you to try these. You can find these puffs in any Asian supermarket and they're deliciously chewy and spongy, soaking up every ounce of nutty, fragrant sauce and bursting in your mouth when you bite into them.

vegetable or extra virgin olive oil
½ white onion, thinly sliced
2 garlic cloves, finely chopped
    or grated
20g fresh ginger, finely chopped
    or grated
½ tsp ground cumin
½ tsp ground coriander
¼ tsp ground cinnamon
3 cardamom pods
200g potatoes, cut into 2.5cm cubes
200ml water
200ml coconut milk
70g tofu puffs, chopped
    in half diagonally
1½ tbsp peanut butter
1 tbsp soy sauce, plus extra to taste
juice of ½ lime
2 tsp brown sugar
salt (optional)

To serve:
salted peanuts, roughly chopped
fresh coriander, chopped (optional)
lime wedge

Heat the oil in a saucepan over a medium heat. Fry the onion, garlic and ginger for a couple of minutes.

Add the cumin, coriander, cinnamon and cardamom to the pan and fry for 2–3 more minutes. Once fragrant, add in the potatoes and water. Pop a lid on the pan and let that simmer over a low heat for 15 minutes until softened.

Add in the coconut milk, tofu puffs, peanut butter, soy sauce, lime juice and sugar and let that simmer gently with the lid off for another 5 minutes, until the sauce has thickened slightly and the potatoes are fully cooked.

Once cooked, taste and season with salt, if using, or more soy sauce, if you prefer. Top with the peanuts and fresh coriander, if using, and serve with a wedge of lime.

USE YOUR LEFTOVER…
coconut milk:
page 70

TOAD IN THE HOLE

In York, growing up, there was a restaurant in an old church where you could order a giant Yorkshire pudding filled with mince, vegetables and gravy. As a child, I was in awe of the enormity of the Yorkshire pudding, overjoyed that this could all be for one person. I get a similar joy from this meal, though its scale does seem slightly more in proportion (sadly). Either way, the Yorkshire pudding remains the focal point of the meal, and the ultimate bringer of comforting joy. You can switch up the vegetables and herbs in this, depending on what you like, or have in, but bear in mind the different cooking times and account for this when chopping them up (e.g. squash takes longer to cook than onions, so chop the squash smaller). I like this with tons of gravy.

Prep Time: 10 minutes
Cook Time: 45 minutes

Preheat the oven to 220°C (200°C fan).

Add the vegetables, if using, to a small baking dish or ovenproof frying pan along with the sausages or chipolatas. Drizzle generously with the olive oil and season with salt and pepper. Bake in the oven for 15 minutes.

While that is baking, prepare the batter. Add the egg and flour to a jug or bowl and whisk together until smooth. Add in the milk and herbs, if using, and whisk again until smooth. Season with salt and pepper, whisk, then leave to the side.

Once the sausages and vegetables are cooked, pour the batter around them, then bake in the oven for another 25–30 minutes or until golden brown and crisp. Serve immediately.

100–150g cubed vegetables of
    your choice – I'd recommend
    butternut squash, potatoes and
    red onions (optional)
2–4 sausages or chipolatas
1 tbsp extra virgin olive oil
salt and black pepper

For the batter:
1 egg
60g plain flour
60ml milk
1 tsp fresh or dried herbs (optional)

USE YOUR LEFTOVER:
sausages:
page 134

RISOTTO CARBONARA

Prep Time: 5 minutes
Cook Time: 35 minutes

As you flick through this book, you may think that my sole aim is to be permanently banned from ever returning to Italy as I modify and adapt classics for my own, and hopefully your, enjoyment. I'm optimistic that a large spoonful of this risotto may atone for any sins, however, as it really is a joy to eat. The silky richness of carbonara is already a top contender in the comfort food contest, but I do believe that, in order to achieve maximum comfort, one must be able to eat the meal with a spoon and, alas, spaghetti does not meet this criterion. Fear not, for my risotto carbonara is all at once silky, rich and spoonable. We may have found a winner.

100g pancetta, cut into 1cm pieces, or bacon lardons
80g arborio rice
350ml water
1 egg, plus 1 egg yolk
35g Parmesan, grated
15g cold butter
salt and black pepper

USE YOUR LEFTOVER ...
egg white:
page 188

Add the pancetta or bacon to a cold saucepan, then place over a medium-high heat. Cook for 8 minutes until golden, crisp and some of the fat has rendered out. Once crisp, you can take a spoon or two of pancetta/bacon out of the pan and leave to the side to scatter over at the end, then add in the dry rice and let that toast in the fat for around 2 minutes.

Slowly start to add the water, about 100ml at a time, stirring frequently and only adding more water when the previous addition has been absorbed. While you're doing this, add the egg, egg yolk, Parmesan and a good grind of pepper to a small bowl and mix together until combined.

Adding the water should take around 18 minutes and by this point the rice should be mostly cooked. Cook until the risotto is slightly thicker than you want the end result to be. Once the water has all been absorbed, take the pan off the heat for 2 minutes, stirring consistently to cool down the mixture slightly.

After 2 minutes, take a spoonful of the risotto and add it to the egg and cheese mix and mix together. This will temper the eggs and prevent them from scrambling. Add the egg mixture to the pan of risotto and mix together well. When combined, put the pan back over a medium-low heat for 2–3 more minutes until the risotto is creamy and silky and slowly falls off a spoon (not too runny and definitely not too thick). Finally, add in the cold butter and mix together until melted.

Season with salt if needed (the Parmesan and pancetta are both salty). Serve with an extra crack of pepper and a scatter of the reserved pancetta/bacon.

CARAMELISED ONION, SQUASH + GOAT'S CHEESE TARTE TATIN

Prep Time: 15 minutes
Cook Time: 60 minutes

Nutty squash, sweet roasted red onions and earthy goat's cheese are the best of friends, held together here by buttery pastry and a sticky, sweet balsamic glaze. You can use any type of goat's cheese, rind on or off, as it will melt into the tart either way. The nuts add a lovely flavour and crunch, but they're optional as the tart is just as delicious without them. Serve with rocket for a peppery freshness to contrast the richness of the tart.

125g butternut squash, peeled and
   cut into 1–2cm semi-circles
½ red onion, thinly sliced
1 tbsp extra virgin olive oil
½ tsp dried thyme, or 2–3 sprigs
   of fresh thyme
75g ready-rolled puff pastry
45g goat's cheese, cut into 1cm cubes
1 tbsp balsamic vinegar
1½ tsp honey
1 tbsp pine nuts/chopped
   pecans (optional)
salt and black pepper

To serve:
rocket leaves

Preheat the oven to 220°C (200°C fan).

Add the squash and onion to a small ovenproof frying pan or baking dish, then add the olive oil, thyme and season with salt and pepper. Mix everything together, then roast for 30 minutes.

While the veg are roasting, unroll the pastry and cut to fit your pan/dish.

Once roasted, scatter the goat's cheese over the squash and onion along with the balsamic and honey and the pine nuts or pecans, if using. Season with a little extra salt and pepper. Mix again, then flatten everything out and place the pastry circle on top of the mixture, tucking it in around the edges. Bake in the oven for another 25–30 minutes or until the pastry is crisp.

Once cooked, take your serving plate and place it face-side down on top of the pan. Flip over the pan to turn out the tart so the vegetables and goat's cheese are now facing up on your plate. Serve with rocket leaves.

USE YOUR LEFTOVER
puff pastry:
page 116

CHILLI CON CARNE CON RICE

Prep Time: 5 minutes
Cook Time: 30 minutes

This chilli is very much inspired by Anna Jones, whose 'all-pleasing chilli', with grains incorporated into the main dish, is very much a staple in the Wilkinson household. Cooking the rice in the chilli not only saves on washing-up but ensures every mouthful is packed with flavour. Eat on its own, or top with sour cream and scoop up with handfuls of salty tortilla chips.

2 tsp extra virgin olive oil

½ white onion, finely chopped

2 garlic cloves, finely
  chopped or grated

125g beef mince

1 tbsp tomato purée

½ tsp ground cumin

½ tsp ground coriander

½–1 tsp chilli powder

¼ tsp ground cinnamon

50g basmati rice

¼ tin kidney beans (60g drained
  weight)

200g tinned tomatoes

250ml water

½ beef stock cube or pot

juice of ½ lime

handful of fresh coriander
  (5–10g), finely chopped

salt and black pepper

To serve:

sour cream

tortilla chips

Heat the oil in a saucepan over a medium heat. Add the onion and a pinch of salt and fry for 4–5 minutes until soft. Add the garlic and cook for another 2–3 minutes. Add in the beef mince and cook for a few minutes until browned.

Add in the tomato purée along with the cumin, ground coriander, chilli (adjusting the quantity to suit your spice preferences), cinnamon and a good crack of pepper. Cook for another 3–4 minutes until the tomato purée is a deep, rich colour and the spices are fragrant.

Rinse the rice in a sieve, then add to the pan along with the kidney beans, tinned tomatoes, water and stock cube or pot. Stir everything together and bring to the boil before turning the heat down to a simmer for around 15 minutes, stirring frequently. Depending on the size of your pan and the heat you're using, you may need to add more water or cook for a few more minutes. You are looking for the rice to be cooked and the chilli to be thick and rich.

Slice off a wedge of lime to serve, then squeeze the rest of the lime into the chilli. Add in most of the chopped coriander, saving a little to garnish. Taste and season with salt and pepper.

Serve with a dollop of sour cream, the rest of the coriander, the wedge of lime and a handful of tortilla chips.

USE YOUR LEFTOVER

beef mince:
page 52

CHICKEN, SWEETCORN + LEEK POT PIE

This pie sparked debate online due to its lack of a pastry bottom. As a northerner myself, part of me mourns the loss of a double hit of pastry, particularly as the soggy bottom really is my favourite part. To avoid further conflict, I have now declared this is a 'pot pie' as opposed to just a 'pie'. Pastry qualms aside, I think chicken, leek and sweetcorn is my number one filling. Visiting grandma when we were young often meant placing orders at the local pie shop for lunch, and I would find myself dismayed that the only chicken pie option would be chicken and mushroom, the vegetable I distance myself from wherever possible. Though I was more than content with my choice of mince and potato pie, I'm glad this chicken pie has also found its place at the table.

Prep Time: 15 minutes
Cook Time: 50 minutes

Preheat the oven to 180°C (160°C fan).

Place the leek in an individual-sized pie dish with the butter, a small sprinkle of salt and a good crack of pepper. Bake in the oven for 20 minutes until the leek is soft.

While the leek is cooking, prep the chicken thigh, if needed. Using your hands, and a knife to help where needed, gently pull the skin off the thigh. To remove the bone, simply cut around, keeping your knife as close to the bone as possible. Don't worry if you cut through the meat, you're going to be cutting up the thigh anyway. Once the bone has been removed, cut the chicken into 2cm pieces.

When the leek is cooked, add the sweetcorn, cornflour, thyme, stock, cream cheese and water to the dish. Whisk everything together with a fork until the cornflour has dissolved. Add in the chicken.

Unroll the pastry and cut it so it is slightly bigger than the pie dish. Place the pastry on top of the filling and seal it by pressing the pastry down around the top rim of the dish. If you have a leftover egg yolk, you could brush it over the pastry now, but this only really adds colour, so don't worry if you don't have it. Cut a small slit in the top to let steam out, then bake in the oven for 30 minutes until the pastry is crisp and golden.

Let it cool slightly before serving.

½ leek, thinly sliced
20g butter
1 skinless, boneless chicken thigh
    (if you can only buy skin-on,
    bone-in thighs, see the method
    for how to remove)
50g tinned or frozen sweetcorn
1 tsp cornflour
½ tsp dried thyme
½ chicken or vegetable stock
    cube or pot
30g cream cheese
100ml water
80–100g ready-rolled
    shortcrust pastry
egg yolk (optional)
salt and black pepper

USE YOUR LEFTOVER...

chicken thigh:
page 82

PRAWN TOASTIE

Prep Time: 15 minutes
Cook Time: 15 minutes

Prawn toast is usually the first thing I reach for out of the takeaway bag, snaffling a piece away as I unpack the rest of the order. Crispy, crunchy and soft all at once, I've taken the essence of this classic, deep-fried bread and reimagined it into a slightly more casual prawn toastie, filled with fresh prawns and spring onions and flavoured with soy, sugar and sesame. When it comes to bread, I do think that soft, cheap, pre-sliced bread really is the way to go here to ensure the correct contrast between soft and crisp, but if you'd like to use local artisan sourdough, I won't stop you.

85g raw peeled prawns
1 spring onion, finely chopped
1 garlic clove, finely chopped
½ tsp soy sauce
½ tsp sugar
pinch of salt
2 slices of bread
sesame oil
2 tsp sesame seeds

To serve:
sweet chilli sauce

Place the prawns on a chopping board and finely chop them, running the knife back and forth until you have a slightly chunky paste. Mix the chopped spring onion and garlic with the prawns using your knife. Add the soy sauce, sugar and a pinch of salt to the prawn mixture and, again, run your knife through to mix everything together.

Take your bread and drizzle each piece with a little sesame oil. Spread the prawn filling on one side of one piece of bread, then place the other piece of bread on top to create a sandwich. Drizzle a little more sesame oil on the top of the sandwich, then sprinkle over half of the sesame seeds. Repeat on the other side of the sandwich with the rest of the seeds.

Heat a frying pan over a medium heat. When hot, add a small drizzle of sesame oil to the pan, then add the sandwich. Put a lid, or a plate, over the pan and cook on one side for 6 minutes, then flip and cook on the other side for 6 minutes, until both sides are golden and toasted and the prawns are cooked.

Serve with sweet chilli sauce.

USE YOUR LEFTOVER
prawns:
page 132

TARRAGON CHICKEN WITH LEEKS, PEAS + POTATOES

Prep Time: 10 minutes
Cook Time: 55 minutes

Tarragon chicken is a French classic and though tarragon may not be the herb you tend to reach for, or at least, it isn't for me, it has the most wonderful fragrant flavour and this creamy sauce wouldn't be the same without it. Spooning the cream over the chicken breast helps the skin crisp up slightly so you get a nice contrast with the vegetables. Feel free to swap the peas for asparagus or green beans or another green veg that is in season.

175g baby potatoes, cut in half
  or into quarters
extra virgin olive oil
½ leek, sliced into 1cm rings
1 skin-on chicken breast
5g fresh tarragon, roughly chopped
3 tbsp white wine
3 tbsp double cream
60g frozen peas
salt and black pepper

Preheat the oven to 195°C (175°C fan).

Add the potatoes to a small ovenproof frying pan or baking dish with a drizzle of olive oil and roast for 15 minutes.

Add the sliced leek to the pan/dish. Season with salt and pepper, then place the chicken breast on top, skin-side facing up. Season this with salt and pepper too.

Sprinkle the tarragon all over the dish. Pour the white wine into the bottom of the pan/dish, then spoon the cream over everything, including the chicken skin.

Roast in the oven for 30 minutes. After 30 minutes, add the peas, sprinkling them around the pan/dish, then roast for a final 10 minutes until the chicken and potatoes are fully cooked and golden.

USE YOUR LEFTOVER:

potatoes and
chicken breast:
page 164

MEATBALL + MOZZARELLA ORZO

This is one of my sister's favourite recipes and I frequently receive messages from her letting me know that she's made it again. I don't blame her, I think it might be one of my favourites too. This dish uses only a handful of ingredients but really emphasises their flavour, so I would recommend buying the best quality meatballs and tinned tomatoes that you can. Salt is really important to bring out the sweet richness of the tomatoes, so season as you go and be generous. Feel free to add fresh or dried chilli too, if you like.

Prep Time: 5 minutes
Cook Time: 40 minutes

Preheat the oven to 200°C (180°C fan).

Start by making the tomato sauce. Melt the butter in a small ovenproof frying pan or baking dish over a medium-low heat. Add in the garlic and cook for a couple of minutes until soft and slightly golden. Add in the tinned tomatoes and the basil and season really well with salt (the salt really brings this together, so taste as you add and be generous). Let that simmer for 5 minutes, then add in the orzo and water.

Give it a good stir, then set the meatballs on top of the orzo and place in the oven for 25 minutes, stirring halfway through but keeping the meatballs on top.

Take the bake out of the oven and give it another stir. You can add a splash more water if it looks like it needs it (it should be slightly looser than you want the final sauce to be). Top with the mozzarella, then bake for another 5–10 minutes on a high shelf in the oven until golden brown. Finish with a scatter of extra basil leaves.

20g butter
2 garlic cloves, finely sliced
200g tinned tomatoes
10g fresh basil, chopped, plus a few extra to garnish
85g orzo
150ml water
1 portion of pork, beef or vegetarian meatballs (3–6 meatballs)
50g mozzarella (drained and dried slightly if using fresh), grated or thinly sliced
salt

USE YOUR LEFTOVER...

meatballs: page 120 (in place of sausages)

HASH BROWN COTTAGE PIE

Prep Time: 10 minutes
Cook Time: 55 minutes

I do think you'd be hard-pressed to find a meal that isn't improved by a hash brown. One of the potato greats, it provides both crisp and fluff as well as a level of structural integrity you may not be afforded by other forms of potato. This is not to disrespect mashed potato, which we love, but rather to provide an equally delicious but less labour-intensive alternative. I'm all about taking the time to properly cook for yourself, but making mashed potato for one is just one step too far. Thank you to our frozen friends for stepping into the role so beautifully.

½ white onion, finely diced

½ carrot, finely diced

extra virgin olive oil

1 garlic clove, finely chopped

1 tbsp tomato purée

100g beef mince

50ml red wine

½ tsp dried mixed herbs

2½ tsp gravy granules

225ml water

50g frozen peas

1 tsp soy sauce

3–4 frozen hash browns

salt and black pepper

To serve:

fresh parsley, finely chopped
    (optional)

Preheat the oven to 190°C (170°C fan).

Sauté the onion and carrot in a small ovenproof frying pan or baking dish with a little olive oil for 8–10 minutes or until soft. Add the garlic to the pan/dish along with the tomato purée once the onion and carrot are soft, then cook for another 2 minutes. Then add the mince and let this brown for a couple of minutes.

When browned, deglaze the pan with the red wine and let that cook off for another 3 minutes. Add in the dried herbs, gravy granules, water, frozen peas and soy sauce. Give everything a mix and simmer for 10 minutes. Taste and season generously with salt and pepper.

Arrange 3 or 4 hash browns on top of the mince, then place in the oven and cook for 30 minutes, or until golden. Sprinkle over the fresh parsley, if using, before serving.

USE YOUR LEFTOVER ...

beef mince:
page 111

MAC + CHEESE WITH CRISPY ONIONS

Prep Time: 5 minutes
Cook Time: 15 minutes

It wouldn't be a comfort chapter without mac and cheese now would it? The epitome of comfort and the meal I crave more than any other. The crispy onions are especially addictive and add a nice little crunch to each bite. They're a great store-cupboard ingredient to have on hand to sprinkle over other meals too. You can switch up the cheeses in this if you like, but you want one strong, sharp cheese, such as Cheddar and one milder, creamier cheese, such as mozzarella. If you're using a different pasta shape, then you may need slightly more milk or water so keep an eye on the pasta as it cooks and adjust if necessary.

20g butter

1 tbsp plain flour

200ml milk

200ml water

¼ tsp Dijon mustard

85g macaroni

35g Cheddar, grated

35g mozzarella, grated

salt and black pepper

To serve:

crispy onions (shop-bought)

Add the butter to a saucepan over a medium heat and let it melt. Stir in the flour and cook off for 2–3 minutes. Slowly pour in the milk, whisking together to create a smooth sauce. Add in the water, mustard and macaroni and season with salt and pepper. Stir everything together and cook for 7–8 minutes, stirring frequently, until the pasta is almost done.

Once the macaroni is almost cooked, turn the heat to low and add in both cheeses. Mix everything together and keep stirring until the cheese has melted and the sauce has thickened. If the sauce becomes too thick, add in a splash more water or milk.

Pour into a bowl and top with crispy onions.

USE YOUR LEFTOVER

mozzarella:
page 73

A chapter that hits every flavour profile, these recipes pack a real punch. Think zingy citrus, spicy chilli and aromatic herbs – you can practically feel the sun beaming down on your face as you flick through these pages. Inspired by flavours from across the world, this chapter includes hot bowls of ginger chicken rice, salmon, coconut and lemongrass noodles and jerk chicken with coconut rice and pineapple, as well as vibrant salads such as my satay slaw with curried chicken skewers, chicken Caesar salad with chicken-fat panko crumbs and pickled vegetable salad with soy-glazed meatballs.

FRESH

PEACH + BURRATA ORZO SALAD

For me, cooking for one is all about joy. The joy of choosing whatever you fancy, the joy of taking the time to make something only you need to find delicious and the joy of eating alone, finding a moment for yourself and your food. This peach and burrata orzo salad is also pure joy. It might only take 20 minutes to make, but for some reason it feels a little special – and you deserve to eat special things. A summer staple for me, juicy, ripe peaches are the stars of the show and, when eaten with creamy burrata (measure with your heart and use as much as you like), are guaranteed to bring happiness.

Prep Time: 10 minutes
Cook Time: 10 minutes

Boil the orzo in a pan of salted water for 7–9 minutes until al dente.

Once cooked, drain the orzo and add to your serving bowl along with the peach, tomatoes, basil and mint. Add a good drizzle of olive oil and the lemon juice and season with salt and pepper. Mix everything together.

Tear as much burrata over the salad as you like, before serving with a final drizzle of olive oil and another sprinkle of salt and a crack of pepper.

85g orzo
1 ripe peach, stoned and thinly sliced
100g cherry tomatoes, cut in half
10g fresh basil, finely chopped
2 sprigs of fresh mint, finely chopped
extra virgin olive oil
juice of ½ lemon
salt and black pepper

To serve:
burrata

USE YOUR LEFTOVER ...

peach:
page 178

COURGETTE CARPACCIO WITH CRISPY CAPERS + BUTTER BEANS

My friend Lauren first introduced me to the joy of courgette salad with bursts of crispy capers hidden throughout, at a dinner party in London. I believe she used a Rick Stein recipe but, unfortunately, he wasn't at dinner so, sorry Rick, but Lauren gets the credit for this one. 'Carpaccio' is really just a fancy way of saying 'thinly sliced', but I'm not sure calling this 'thinly sliced courgette' would really convince anyone to make it. But you should make this! It's fresh and light and the creamy ricotta is a lovely contrast with the crispy capers, beans and breadcrumbs. Use a nice juicy lemon and be sure to scoop it all up with handfuls of crusty bread.

Prep Time: 10 minutes
Cook Time: 10 minutes

Add the olive oil to a frying pan over a medium-high heat and fry the capers and butter beans for around 5 minutes until crisp. Add in the breadcrumbs and fry for another couple of minutes until golden. Season with salt and pepper.

Spread the ricotta over your plate, then layer over the courgette. Squeeze over the lemon juice, then spoon over the crispy bean and caper mixture. You could also grate over some lemon zest, if you fancy.

Serve with the bread to scoop it all up.

2 tbsp extra virgin olive oil
2 tbsp capers
½ tin butter beans
   (120g drained weight)
2 tbsp panko breadcrumbs
4–5 tbsp ricotta
1 small courgette, thinly sliced
juice of 1 lemon
salt and black pepper

To serve:
crusty bread

USE YOUR LEFTOVER

butter beans:
page 100

CHICKEN CAESAR SALAD WITH CHICKEN-FAT PANKO CRUMBS

Prep Time: 5 minutes
Cook Time: 20 minutes

Salads can get a bad rap – limp leaves, lack of any real flavour, unsatisfying and unsatiating. So, for anyone who still needs convincing, I urge you to make this Caesar salad. A punchy dressing packed with lemon, mustard, anchovies and garlic. Golden chicken perched atop crisp lettuce with lashings of Parmesan. And most importantly, the chicken-fat panko. Where awkward overly-crunchy croutons would usually sit, I've swapped in these panko breadcrumbs, which distribute the crunch evenly through every bite, adding both texture and flavour. Not bad for a humble crumb.

1 chicken breast or thigh, skin on
1 tbsp extra virgin olive oil
75–100g baby gem lettuce,
  cut into strips
20g Parmesan, grated
2 tbsp panko breadcrumbs
salt and black pepper

For the dressing:
1 tbsp mayonnaise
1 tbsp lemon juice
¼ tsp Dijon mustard
2 anchovies
1 small garlic clove, grated
10g Parmesan, grated

Season the chicken with salt and pepper, then heat the oil in a frying pan over a medium heat. Place the chicken in the pan, skin-side down, and cook for 12–15 minutes until cooked, turning halfway through.

While the chicken is cooking, prepare the salad dressing. Add the mayonnaise, lemon juice and mustard to a serving bowl. Finely chop the anchovies, then use the flat side of your knife to crush them into a paste. Add this to the bowl with the garlic and the 10g of Parmesan for the dressing. Mix everything together to create your Caesar dressing.

Add the lettuce to the bowl. Toss together with the dressing and sprinkle over the remaining 20g of Parmesan.

Once the chicken is cooked, take it out of the pan, slice it and place it on top of the salad. Keep the pan on the heat but turn the heat to low. There should be some fat left over in the pan, but if there isn't much, add another small drizzle of olive oil. Add the panko breadcrumbs to the pan and toast for 2–3 minutes until golden. Sprinkle over the salad before serving.

USE YOUR LEFTOVER...
chicken breast:
page 104

GINGER CHICKEN RICE BOWL

Prep Time: 10 minutes
Cook Time: 20 minutes

Usually I would consider a brothy meal that you eat with a bowl and a spoon a form of comfort food, however, the flavours in this dish are so fresh and vibrant that it has to go in this chapter. I love the fiery freshness of ginger and it's the predominant flavour in this rich chicken broth. The finished dish isn't a soup as such, but there is just enough broth to make every mouthful deliciously juicy. It also takes minimal time to make so it's a useful recipe to have on hand for days when you're short of time.

---

1 tbsp sesame oil, plus extra to serve

2 garlic cloves, finely sliced

10g fresh ginger, chopped
   into matchsticks

300ml water

½ chicken stock pot

1 tsp soy sauce

1 tsp rice wine vinegar

55g basmati rice

1 chicken breast, cut into
   2cm-thick slices

55g broccoli (regular or
   Tenderstem), chopped into
   small pieces

5g fresh coriander, finely chopped

1 spring onion, thinly sliced
   at an angle

salt (optional)

In a pan, heat the sesame oil over a medium heat. Fry the garlic and ginger until they have softened slightly and smell fragrant but haven't coloured too much.

Add in the water, stock pot, soy sauce and rice wine vinegar. Bring to a simmer and taste – if needed, add a little salt. Bring to the boil, then add in the basmati rice and cook for 5 minutes.

After 5 minutes, turn the heat down to a gentle simmer and add in the chicken and broccoli (tenderstem broccoli will take slightly less time, so add this in when you only have 4–5 minutes left). Put a lid on and cook for 8 minutes. You want it to stay at a gentle simmer so the chicken poaches but doesn't toughen.

Place the coriander and spring onion slices in your serving bowl. Once the chicken and rice are cooked, spoon into the bowl with the coriander and spring onion and mix together. Finish with a final drizzle of sesame oil to serve.

USE YOUR LEFTOVER
chicken breast:
page 22

CURRIED GNOCCHI, CORN + TOMATO BAKE

Sweetcorn is my favourite vegetable and, when roasted and slightly charred, gives a real nuttiness that adds another dimension to the sweet kernels. I've combined this with crispy curried gnocchi, blistered tomatoes and broccoli, though you could try different vegetables if you wanted. You could use any curry paste for this, or natural yoghurt instead of coconut yoghurt, though the slight coconut sweetness really does add something a little extra.

Prep Time: 5 minutes
Cook Time: 20 minutes

Preheat the grill to 225°C.

Add the oil to a large ovenproof frying pan or small roasting tray, then add the gnocchi, tomatoes, corn and broccoli to the pan. Add the curry paste and a pinch of salt and pepper. Mix everything together, making sure all the veg are covered in the curry paste. Grill for 17 minutes, until everything starts to char slightly, and the tomatoes are beginning to burst.

After 17 minutes, add in the cashews and grill for a final 3 minutes.

Squeeze over the lemon juice, then plate up. Spoon over the coconut yoghurt and sprinkle over the coriander to serve.

2 tsp extra virgin olive oil
150g gnocchi
100g cherry tomatoes
1 corn on the cob, cut into 6 pieces
100g broccoli, chopped into
　　small pieces
3 tbsp tikka masala curry paste
30g cashews, roughly chopped
juice of ½ lemon
salt and black pepper

To serve:
2–3 tbsp coconut yoghurt
10g fresh coriander,
　　roughly chopped

USE YOUR LEFTOVER ...

gnocchi:
page 119

HERBY CHICKEN + RICE SALAD

Prep Time: 10 minutes
Cook Time: 20 minutes

This is a meal I make again and again and it has everything I could possibly want from a salad. You can eat this as soon as it's ready, while it's still warm (I prefer it like this, the flavours really sing), or let it cool and keep it in the fridge until you need it. Poaching the chicken gives a tender, juicy result, but be careful not to have the heat too high, as boiling can toughen the meat, so keep it on a very gentle simmer until fully cooked.

1 litre water

1 chicken stock cube

1 large chicken breast

75g basmati rice, rinsed

¼ small red onion
  (approx. 20g), finely sliced

2 tsp white wine vinegar

5g fresh coriander, finely chopped

5g fresh mint, finely chopped

3 tbsp pomegranate seeds

2 tbsp cashews or pine nuts,
  roughly chopped

juice of ½ lemon

1 tsp extra virgin olive oil

salt

To serve:

2 tbsp coconut yoghurt

Fill a pan with the water and add in the stock cube. Bring to the boil over a high heat then, once boiling, turn down to a very low heat until the water is barely simmering. Place the whole chicken breast in the water and gently poach for 5 minutes. Add the rice to the water and continue to simmer for another 10 minutes until both are cooked.

Meanwhile, add the onion to your serving bowl along with the white wine vinegar. This will lightly pickle the onion.

Once the chicken and rice are done, take the chicken out and place on your chopping board, then drain the rice and add it to your serving bowl along with the herbs, pomegranate seeds, nuts, lemon juice and olive oil. Shred the chicken using two forks or your hands, then add this to the bowl too, and mix. Season well with salt and serve with dollops of coconut yoghurt.

USE YOUR LEFTOVER ⋮

coconut yoghurt:
page 67

SALMON, COCONUT + LEMONGRASS NOODLES

Prep Time: 10 minutes
Cook Time: 15 minutes

I don't use lemongrass as often as I should, but when I do I'm reminded of its citrusy, aromatic fragrance and flavour which pairs beautifully with rich, creamy coconut milk and earthy turmeric. Buying lemongrass paste makes for a handy hack as the fibrous stalks of fresh lemongrass can be fiddly to prepare. If you are using fresh lemongrass, I find grating the stalk with a microplane grater the easiest way to do it and you can grate the garlic and ginger at the same time.

1 tsp extra virgin olive oil

2 garlic cloves, finely grated

15g fresh ginger, finely grated

1 tbsp lemongrass paste or 1
    lemongrass stalk, finely grated

½ tsp ground turmeric

200ml coconut milk

100ml water

1 tsp soy sauce

1 skinless salmon fillet, cut into
    4cm pieces

40g mangetout, ends trimmed

1 packet of udon noodles

salt

To serve:

5g fresh coriander, finely chopped

Heat the olive oil in a pan over a medium heat. Gently fry off the garlic, ginger, lemongrass and turmeric for 3 minutes or until fragrant. Add in the coconut milk, water and soy sauce and bring to a gentle simmer. Taste and season with more soy sauce or salt as desired.

Add in the salmon and the mangetout and gently poach for 4 minutes, then add the noodles and cook for another 2–3 minutes until soft.

Sprinkle over the fresh coriander and serve.

USE YOUR LEFTOVER ...

salmon fillet:
page 114

CHICKEN, MANGO + AVOCADO TACOS WITH LIME CREMA

This might be one of my favourite recipes in this chapter. Spiced chicken, sweet mango, creamy avocado, toasted tacos and melted mozzarella – need I say more?! The lime crema and fresh coriander bring everything together to create a flavour sensation that's satisfying and comforting while still feeling fresh. Pineapple would also be yummy in place of the mango, if you prefer.

Prep Time: 15 minutes
Cook Time: 10 minutes

Heat the oil in a large frying pan over a medium heat. Fry the chicken for 2 minutes, then add in the garlic, paprika, cumin and coriander and season with salt and pepper. Cook for 3 more minutes until the chicken is just cooked, then turn off the heat.

Take your serving plate and lay out the tacos. Place one-third of the mozzarella on one side of each taco shell. Spoon the chicken on top of the cheese, distributing it evenly across the three tacos. Do the same with the mango, placing it on top of the chicken. Add a sprinkle of fresh coriander to each taco, leaving some to serve at the end, then fold the empty half of the taco shell over the top of the filling.

Put your pan over a medium heat again. There should be some residual oil in the pan (along with some of the spices), but add a little more if necessary so the tacos don't stick. Place the tacos in the pan and cook for 2 minutes until the bottom is golden and crisp. Flip over and cook for another 2 minutes on the other side.

While they're cooking, for the lime crema, mix the sour cream with the lime juice in a little pot and season with a pinch of salt.

Plate up the tacos and place a couple of avocado slices inside each one. Sprinkle over the remaining coriander and dip the tacos in the lime crema before eating.

2 tsp extra virgin olive oil
1 chicken breast, cut into 2cm cubes
1 garlic clove, finely chopped
   or grated
½ tsp paprika
½ tsp ground cumin
½ tsp ground coriander
3 soft shell or corn tacos
45g mozzarella, grated
½ small ripe mango (approx. 75g),
   peeled and cut into 1cm cubes
5g fresh coriander, finely chopped
½ avocado, cut into 1cm slices
salt and black pepper

For the lime crema:
2 tbsp sour cream
juice of ½ lime

USE YOUR LEFTOVER...

mango:
page 200

ROASTED RED PEPPER, TOMATO + PRESERVED LEMON ORZO

Prep Time: 10 minutes
Cook Time: 45 minutes

Orzo is fast becoming my go-to pasta shape. It retains a great bite that you don't always get with other one-pot pastas and, because it's small, you end up getting a bit of everything on your fork which maximises flavour. If you haven't tried preserved lemons before then please do, as their wonderful flavour and soft, jammy texture is entirely distinct from fresh lemon, plus the jar will keep for ages in your cupboard. Add to soups and stews for an extra zing.

½ red pepper, cut into 2cm dice

100g cherry tomatoes, cut in half

10g preserved lemon (rind only), finely diced

1 garlic clove, thinly sliced

20g pitted green olives, cut in half

8–10 fresh basil leaves, plus extra to garnish

1 tsp balsamic vinegar

extra virgin olive oil

75g orzo

200ml water

salt

Preheat the oven to 200°C (180°C fan).

Add the red pepper, tomatoes, preserved lemon, garlic, olives, basil and vinegar to a small ovenproof frying pan or baking dish, then add a generous glug of oil and season well with salt. Bake for 20 minutes or until the tomatoes and pepper have softened.

Add in the orzo and water and another pinch of salt, then mix everything together and bake for another 20–25 minutes. Depending on the size of your pan/dish, you may need to add another splash of water during the cooking, but at the end you should be left with al dente orzo in a loose, but not watery, sauce. Mix everything well together again, as this releases the starches to create a silky sauce. Garnish with basil leaves and serve.

USE YOUR LEFTOVER:
red pepper and tomatoes:
page 81

CHILAQUILES WITH EGG + FETA

Prep Time: 10 minutes
Cook Time: 40 minutes

Chilaquiles is a traditional breakfast dish from Mexico that is often found in two varieties: chilaquiles rojos, which uses a tomato and chilli-based sauce (my version is inspired by this), and chilaquiles verdes, which uses a herby tomatillo salsa. Usually, the tortillas are fried but I've baked them instead, purely for ease and to keep this dish one-pot. Corn tortillas are traditional but flour tortillas are easier to find so I often use those instead. Either work and both are delicious.

1 large, or 2 small, tortilla wraps, cut into triangles
extra virgin olive oil
½ white onion, grated or finely chopped
2 garlic cloves, grated or finely chopped
1 red chilli, finely chopped
200g tinned tomatoes
30g mozzarella, grated
30g feta cheese, crumbled
1 egg
salt

To serve:
sour cream (optional)
fresh coriander and/or chives, roughly chopped (optional)

Preheat the oven to 200°C (180°C fan).

Place the tortilla triangles in a small ovenproof frying pan or dish. Drizzle with olive oil and season with salt. Bake for 15 minutes.

Once the tortilla pieces are golden, take the pan out of the oven and sprinkle over the onion, garlic and chilli. Spoon the tinned tomatoes over the top of this and add 2 tablespoons of water. Season generously with salt. Stir the tomatoes and onion together slightly, then sprinkle both types of cheese on top of the tomato mixture, leaving a little circle in the middle where the egg will go.

Bake for 10 minutes, then take it out of the oven, crack the egg into the centre, season with a little more salt and bake for another 10–15 minutes or until the egg is cooked to your liking.

Top with sour cream and/or fresh herbs to serve.

USE YOUR LEFTOVER...

tinned tomatoes:
page 42

PICKLED VEGETABLE SALAD WITH SOY-GLAZED MEATBALLS

Prep Time: 20 minutes
Cook Time: 10 minutes

Inspired by the flavours of bánh mì, specifically bánh mì xíu mai, this salad is jam-packed with fresh herbs and crunchy vegetables and, because the substance of the salad comes from vegetables as opposed to leaves, it satiates without feeling heavy. Though traditionally a sandwich, here I've kept things light and fresh but, if you want to stick this in a crusty baguette, by all means be my guest. The sticky glazed meatballs bring everything together to complete the meal, just be sure to add the glaze at the end so as not to burn it.

For the salad:

1 carrot, chopped into ½cm wide batons

100g cucumber, deseeded and chopped into ½cm wide batons

½–1 red chilli, thinly sliced into semi-circles

5g fresh coriander, finely chopped

2 tbsp rice wine vinegar

1 tsp caster sugar

1 tsp sesame oil

salt

For the meatballs:

180g pork mince (around 20% fat)

1–2 tsp sesame oil

3 tsp soy sauce

1 tsp caster sugar

salt and black pepper

To serve:

1 spring onion, finely sliced

Place the carrot, cucumber, chilli and coriander in your serving bowl. Add the rice wine vinegar, sugar and sesame oil and toss together with the vegetables, then taste and season with salt. Leave the vegetables to pickle slightly while you prep the meatballs.

Take your pork mince and roll into nine 20g meatballs, squishing the mince together as you roll so that the meatballs are tender and compact.

Heat the sesame oil in a small frying pan over a medium-low heat, then add the meatballs and season well with salt and pepper. Fry for 8–10 minutes, or until cooked through with a nice colour on the outside. Once cooked, add in the soy sauce and sugar and cook for a final 2 minutes to reduce the glaze and coat the meatballs.

Add the meatballs to the salad and spoon over any remaining glaze. Sprinkle over the spring onion before serving.

USE YOUR LEFTOVER ...
pork mince:
page 94

HALLOUMI OR COD PROVENÇAL

I'm a huge fan of the briny salinity of capers and olives and the depth and zing they bring to a dish like this one. I make this Provençal either with flaky cod (or another firm white fish) or halloumi, which makes for a great vegetarian version. Either way, it's essential that you serve this with plenty of crusty bread to mop up the rich juices.

Prep Time: 10 minutes
Cook Time: 30 minutes

Preheat the oven to 200°C (180°C fan).

Add the cherry tomatoes, olives and red pepper to an ovenproof frying pan or baking dish along with the capers, olive oil and herbs. Add the white wine and season well with salt and pepper. Mix everything together, then roast in the oven for 20 minutes.

After 20 minutes, the veg should have softened. Place the halloumi or cod on top of the vegetables and season with salt (you will need to season slightly less for the halloumi). Drizzle a little extra olive oil over the top, then add a drizzle of honey.

Roast for another 10 minutes for the cod, 15 minutes for he halloumi.

Serve with a hunk of crusty bread.

100g cherry tomatoes, cut in half
40g pitted green olives, cut
   in half
½ red pepper, chopped into small
   pieces
1 tbsp capers
1 tbsp extra virgin olive oil, plus
   a little extra for drizzling
3 sprigs of fresh thyme or sage
60ml white wine
100g halloumi or 1 piece of cod
drizzle of honey
salt and black pepper

To serve:
crusty bread

USE YOUR LEFTOVER:
cod:
page 30

JERK CHICKEN WITH COCONUT RICE + PINEAPPLE

Prep Time: 10 minutes
Cook Time: 35 minutes

Who said chicken and rice had to be boring? This tongue-tingling twist on a classic combination is a vibrant concoction of flavours and aromas. Inspired by intricate flavours from Jamaica and the Caribbean, the jerk seasoning brings a hot, smoky, slightly tangy depth to the dish. When combined with fluffy coconut rice and sweet pineapple, this dish is a certified stomach-satisfier. Top with extra fresh chilli if you're feeling spicy.

1 large chicken thigh, skin-on

75g basmati rice, rinsed

75g pineapple, tinned or fresh, cut into small chunks

¼ tin kidney beans (60g drained weight)

150ml coconut milk

50ml pineapple juice from the tin, or water if using fresh pineapple

1 tbsp jerk seasoning paste

salt

To serve:
thinly sliced cucumber
sliced fresh chilli (optional)

Preheat the oven to 220°C (200°C fan).

Place your chicken thigh in a small, cold, ovenproof frying pan, skin-side down, then heat over a medium heat. Once it starts sizzling, cook for 5–6 minutes to render out the fat slightly. Season with salt.

Once the chicken skin has turned golden brown, turn off the heat and remove the thigh, placing it on a chopping board. There will be some chicken fat in the pan, so add the rice to this and stir gently to coat. Add in the pineapple chunks, kidney beans, coconut milk and pineapple juice/water and season well with salt. Stir everything together, then place the chicken thigh on top of the mixture, skin-side up. Spoon the jerk paste on top of the skin and use the back of the spoon to cover the skin with the paste. Cook in the oven for 30 minutes.

After 30 minutes, remove from the oven and serve with the sliced cucumber on the side and scattered with fresh chilli, if using.

USE YOUR LEFTOVER:
coconut milk:
page 92

SATAY SLAW WITH CURRIED CHICKEN SKEWERS

Prep Time: 25 minutes
Cook Time: 10 minutes

I have an affinity for crunchy slaws, as I think they provide more interest, more texture and are more filling than many other salads. However, I'm not partial to excessive quantities of mayonnaise. Here I opt for coconut milk instead, which delivers the same creaminess in a less monotonous way. The fresh coriander and bite of roasted peanuts keep this slaw lively and interesting and are perfect with the lightly charred curried chicken skewers. This would also be great sandwiched between a burger bun, or on a soft flatbread.

For the slaw:
5 tbsp coconut milk
1½ tbsp crunchy peanut butter
juice of 1 lime
¼ tsp curry powder
1 tsp honey
2 tsp soy sauce
½ apple, cored and finely sliced
125g red or white cabbage,
    finely sliced
½–1 red chilli, finely sliced
10g fresh coriander, finely chopped
salt

For the skewers:
1 chicken breast, sliced into strips
1 tsp curry powder
1–2 tsp honey
salt and black pepper
3 wooden skewers

To serve:
handful of roasted peanuts,
    chopped (optional)

Preheat the grill to 200°C.

Start by making your slaw. Add the coconut milk, peanut butter, half of the lime juice, the curry powder, honey and soy sauce to your serving bowl and mix everything together. Season with salt.

Add the apple, cabbage, chilli and coriander to the bowl. Mix together until the slaw is fully coated in the dressing.

For the skewers, sprinkle the chicken strips with the curry powder and honey and season with salt and pepper. Use your hands to mix and spread this evenly over the chicken, then piece by piece thread the chicken strips onto the wooden skewers, creating almost flat ribbons of chicken.

Grill for 5 minutes on each side until the chicken is golden and lightly charred. Place on top of the slaw to serve and squeeze over the remaining lime juice, then sprinkle with the peanuts, if using.

USE YOUR LEFTOVER:
chicken and
coriander:
page 73

PORK + PINEAPPLE FLATBREAD

Prep Time: 10 minutes
Cook Time: 10 minutes

I'll admit that I don't often reach for pork chops as I'm never truly convinced that the end result won't be dry or chewy. Perhaps I've had bad experiences before, but this recipe has changed that narrative for me. The filling in this flatbread is juicy and tender, the pork and pineapple gain a slight char and I adore the sweet, spicy glaze. Tinned and fresh pineapple both work well here, though if using tinned, ensure you buy it in juice as opposed to syrup and use this juice in your glaze.

1 pork chop, fat trimmed,
   cut into 4cm cubes
extra virgin olive oil
75g tinned pineapple rings in juice
   (or fresh pineapple cut into pieces)
½ tbsp gochujang paste
½ tbsp honey
3 tbsp pineapple juice from the tin
   (or water)
salt and black pepper

To serve:
1 Greek-style flatbread
natural yoghurt
handful of fresh coriander, shredded

Add the pork cubes to a cold frying pan with a little olive oil. Place over a high heat, and once it starts sizzling, cook for 2 minutes before adding in the pineapple. Season with salt and pepper and cook for around 5 minutes until both the pineapple and the pork are slightly charred and the pork is fully cooked.

Lightly toast the flatbread, place on a serving plate, then spoon the pork and pineapple over the top. Return the pan to the heat and turn down to low. Add the gochujang paste, honey and pineapple juice or water, stir together and cook until slightly reduced to a thick glaze.

Spoon the glaze over the flatbread, then serve with a few dollops of natural yoghurt and a sprinkle of shredded coriander.

USE YOUR LEFTOVER...
pineapple:
page 82

CHIPOTLE PULLED CHICKEN WITH AVOCADO + TOMATO SALSA + TORTILLA CHIPS

Pulled chicken is my new favourite thing and this bowl is a level up from your standard fajita night. I wouldn't blame you if the thought of poaching meat conjures up images of anaemic, boiled chicken, but I promise this is packed with juicy flavour, thanks to the chipotle – a smoky chilli and the tomato base. Keep the heat low so as not to toughen the meat, then scoop this up with salty tortilla chips and zesty salsa.

Prep Time: 20 minutes
Cook Time: 40 minutes

Place a spoonful of the onion in your serving bowl for the salsa. Add a little olive oil to a small saucepan, then sauté the rest of the onion for around 5 minutes until soft. Next, add the garlic to the onion in the pan and cook for another 2 minutes. Season with salt, then add in the chipotle paste and tomato purée and cook for another 3–4 minutes.

Add the diced tomato to the pan along with the mixed herbs and water. Season with salt and pepper, then bring to the boil and let this bubble away for around 5 minutes.

Turn the heat down to a very gentle simmer, then add in the chicken breast. Let this gently poach for 25 minutes, making sure the heat doesn't get too hot so as not to toughen the chicken.

While the chicken is poaching, make the salsa. Add the tomatoes and avocado to the reserved onion in your serving bowl. Squeeze over the lime juice and a generous drizzle of olive oil. Add the coriander, then taste and season with salt and pepper.

When the chicken is cooked and the sauce has thickened, use two forks to pull the chicken into shreds. Mix with the cooking sauce, then spoon into your bowl with the salsa. Serve with tortilla chips for scooping.

½ red onion, finely diced
extra virgin olive oil
3 garlic cloves, finely chopped
4 tsp chipotle paste
1 tbsp tomato purée
1 large vine tomato, finely diced
½ tsp dried mixed herbs
250ml water
1 chicken breast (sliced in half horizontally if large)
salt and black pepper

For the salsa:
2 large vine tomatoes, finely diced
½ avocado, peeled, stoned and finely diced
juice of 1 lime
extra virgin olive oil
small handful of fresh coriander, finely chopped
salt and black pepper

To serve:
tortilla chips

USE YOUR LEFTOVER

chicken breast: page 104

PEANUT NOODLE SALAD

Prep Time: 15 minutes
Cook Time: 5 minutes

I'm determined to change the rhetoric, which I subscribed to for many years, that salads are bland and boring. They're just misunderstood! The key to unlocking maximum flavour is in the dressing and this one hits every flavour profile; utilising sour lime, salty soy and fish sauce, sweet honey and savoury sesame. Add the crunch of roasted peanuts and raw vegetables and the result is a taste and texture sensation.

1 nest of rice noodles
½ carrot, finely sliced or peeled
   into ribbons
½ red pepper, finely sliced
1 red chilli, finely sliced
5g fresh coriander, finely chopped
5g fresh mint, finely chopped
30g roasted salted peanuts,
   roughly chopped

For the dressing:
2 tsp sesame oil
3 tsp soy sauce
1 tsp rice wine vinegar
splash of fish sauce
1½ tsp honey
juice of ½ lime
5g fresh ginger, grated

To serve:
½ avocado, sliced

Put your rice noodles in a heatproof serving bowl and cover with boiling water. Leave for 3–5 minutes until soft, then drain in a sieve. Rinse the noodles with cold water to stop them sticking together, then leave them in the sieve while you make the dressing.

Add all the ingredients for the dressing to the bowl. Whisk together, then add your rice noodles back to the bowl.

Add the carrot, red pepper, chilli, herbs and the peanuts to the bowl and toss together.

Serve with sliced avocado.

USE YOUR LEFTOVER ...

avocado:
page 129

GREEN CURRY COCONUT RICE

Prep Time: 15 minutes
Cook Time: 40 minutes

The versatility of rice never fails to impress me and here I love the rich, silky result you get from baking it in coconut milk. This recipe calls for fresh veg and protein and, while I've suggested tofu or chicken, really this would work with anything and is also the perfect way to utilise leftover vegetables. How much curry paste you use will depend slightly on the brand that you buy, though if in doubt, I would usually suggest using more – no such thing as too much flavour!

75g basmati rice, rinsed

200ml coconut milk

55ml water

1–2 tbsp Thai green curry paste

150g stir fry vegetables (I like broccoli and baby corn), chopped into 3cm pieces

100g tofu, or 1 chicken breast, chopped into 3cm pieces

30g cashews, roughly chopped

drizzle of sesame oil

soy sauce, to taste

small handful of fresh Thai basil or coriander leaves (optional)

salt

Preheat the oven to 200°C (180°C fan).

Add the rice to a small ovenproof frying pan or baking dish. Add the coconut milk, water and curry paste and mix together. Add the vegetables and the tofu or chicken to the pan/dish. Season with salt and mix together. Bake for 25 minutes.

Take the pan/dish out of the oven and sprinkle the cashews on top, then bake for another 15 minutes.

Once cooked, fluff up the rice with a fork, then drizzle with sesame oil and season with soy sauce. Finish with a sprinkling of fresh herbs, if using, and serve.

USE YOUR LEFTOVER...
coconut milk:
page 130

PORK + GINGER LETTUCE WRAPS

Prep Time: 10 minutes
Cook Time: 15 minutes

Gone are the days when lettuce wraps were merely tasteless, deconstructed salads. Inspired by Thai Larb, these lettuce wraps are filled with the most flavourful pork mince, fragrant with ginger, garlic, chilli, fresh herbs and lime juice. Simultaneously light and zingy, with fiery depth from the fresh ginger and a savoury hit from soy and fish sauces, these wraps are versatile enough for winter warmth or summer salad season. If you want to make these more filling, you can add in some rice with the filling – I'm a huge advocate of microwaveable rice and always have a bag in the cupboard.

sesame oil

½ white onion, finely chopped

150g pork mince (or use beef or vegetarian mince)

3 garlic cloves, finely chopped

10g fresh ginger, finely chopped

½–1 red chilli, finely chopped

100g pre-cooked rice (optional)

1–2 tsp soy sauce

½ tsp fish sauce

5g fresh coriander, finely chopped

5g fresh mint, finely chopped

To serve:

large lettuce leaves (e.g. butterhead, romaine, gem or iceberg)

½ lime

Add a drizzle of sesame oil to a frying pan over a medium heat. Fry the onion for 3–4 minutes, then add in the pork mince and fry until browned slightly. Add in the garlic, ginger and chilli and also the rice, if using. Fry for another 3–4 minutes until fragrant.

Add in the soy sauce, fish sauce and fresh herbs and mix together. Taste and season with more soy sauce if needed.

Spoon the mince mixture into the lettuce leaves to serve and finish with a squeeze of lime.

USE YOUR LEFTOVER ...

pork mince:
page 78

The chapter for days when you have no time, money or thinking space to spare, these recipes are either especially quick to make or require minimal fresh ingredients. This chapter takes the stress out of cooking while still giving you the satisfaction of a homemade meal. I've levelled up weeknight classics, such as my loaded jacket potato and fish finger sandwich, next to new staples for me, such as my vegetable pancake with a chilli crisp egg, brothy pasta with beans and greens, and my smash burger flatbread.

SIMPLE

VEGETABLE PANCAKE WITH A CHILLI CRISP EGG

Prep Time: 15 minutes
Cook Time: 15 minutes

This vegetable pancake has its origin in Korea (where they're known as yachaejeon) and is the perfect dish to use up odds and ends of any vegetables you have lying around. Cabbage, spring onions, carrots and courgettes work really well and provide a nice balance of moisture and crunch, but peppers, potatoes, mushrooms or leafy greens are good alternatives. Depending on the vegetables you use, you may need more or less water to make the light batter so adjust as necessary.

200g vegetables (e.g. 50g carrot, 50g spring onion, 50g cabbage, 50g courgette), sliced into matchstick-sized pieces
60g plain flour
2 tsp sesame seeds
1 tsp soy sauce
1 tsp rice wine vinegar
big pinch of salt
at least 60g water
2 tbsp sesame oil
2 tsp chilli oil
1 egg

To serve:
sriracha, sweet chilli sauce or soy sauce and rice wine vinegar mix

Add the vegetables to a bowl along with the flour, sesame seeds, soy sauce, rice wine vinegar, salt and the water. Stir this all together until well combined. You are looking for every piece of vegetable to be lightly coated in batter, so if any are looking a bit dry you can add some more water. This will depend on the vegetables you use and how much moisture they have.

Grab a large frying pan and add the sesame oil. Let this heat gently over a medium heat, then add in the vegetable mixture. Press it down into a flat layer in the pan and let it cook for 5 minutes on one side. After 5 minutes, it should be golden brown and crisp on the bottom, so take a spatula and quickly but confidently flip the pancake over. Cook for another 5 minutes on the other side until it's also golden and crisp.

Once cooked, tip or flip the pancake onto a plate and put the frying pan back on the heat. The pancake will crisp slightly as it cools. Meanwhile, add the chilli oil to the pan and crack the egg on top. Fry for a few minutes until cooked to your liking, then place on top of the pancake.

You can finish this with sriracha or sweet chilli sauce, or make a dipping sauce with equal parts of soy sauce and rice wine vinegar.

USE YOUR LEFTOVER

vegetables:
page 108 (for the
stir fry)

BROTHY PASTA WITH BEANS + GREENS

Prep Time: 5 minutes
Cook Time: 30 minutes

My take on the Italian classic, 'pasta e fagioli', meaning pasta and beans (or 'pasta e ceci' if you decide to use chickpeas), this broth is comfort maximised. The hint of chilli adds a lovely warmth without too much heat and the grated Parmesan makes the broth silky and rich. It's hearty and satisfying without being heavy, and adding a tangle of green leaves brightens it up. Depending on the shape of pasta you use, you may need to add more water, so keep an eye on it and loosen if needed.

1 tbsp extra virgin olive oil
½ white onion, finely diced
2 garlic cloves, finely sliced
2 tsp tomato purée
¼ tsp dried mixed herbs
¼ tsp chilli flakes
80g short pasta (e.g. macaroni, rigatoni, ditalini)
½ tin cannellini beans, chickpeas or butter beans (100–120g drained weight)
500ml water
½ vegetable stock cube or pot
25g Parmesan, grated
handful of spinach leaves or other leafy greens
salt and black pepper

Heat a saucepan over a medium-low heat, then add the olive oil and onion and fry for around 5 minutes until soft and translucent.

Once soft, add in the garlic and cook for 2 more minutes, then add in the tomato purée, mixed herbs and chilli flakes. Cook for another 2–3 minutes, then add in the pasta, beans or chickpeas, water and stock cube. Bring to the boil, then reduce to a low boil and let it cook for 15 minutes, stirring every few minutes. You can add more water if needed as it cooks.

The pasta should be cooked after 15 minutes, so turn off the heat and add in the Parmesan and the spinach or other green leaves. Stir until the cheese has melted and the spinach has wilted, then taste and season with salt and pepper before serving.

USE YOUR LEFTOVER

cannellini beans: page 61 (in place of butter beans)

CHORIZO, POTATO + FETA FRITTATA

Prep Time: 10 minutes
Cook Time: 15 minutes

Where would we be without eggs?! Probably somewhere sad and hungry. You can whip up this frittata for breakfast, lunch or dinner and it's cheap, quick and satisfying. If you don't eat or enjoy chorizo, you can substitute this with peas and mint for an equally delicious vegetarian frittata. Or combine both! I certainly won't stop you. I recommend making this in a small frying pan so your frittata is slightly softer in the centre, but if you only have a large pan, you could use that too. The result will be more like an omelette and it will be quicker to cook, so adjust the cooking time as necessary.

1 tbsp extra virgin olive oil
150g potatoes, cut into 1cm cubes
3 eggs
40g chorizo, sliced (or substitute with 50g frozen peas + ¼ tsp dried mint for a vegetarian frittata)
salt and black pepper

To serve:
30g feta cheese
fresh mint leaves (optional)

Heat a small frying pan over a high heat and add the olive oil. Add the potatoes, season with salt, then cook with a lid on for 8–9 minutes, stirring occasionally. The potatoes will steam slightly while they crisp up.

Crack the eggs into a bowl, season with salt and pepper and whisk together.

Once the potatoes are done, add the chorizo and cook for another 2–3 minutes (if you're making the pea version, add the peas and dried mint instead). Turn the heat down to medium and add the eggs to the pan. Pop a lid back on and cook until the egg is fully set and there is little to no runny egg on top. Depending on the size and shape of your pan, this could take 1–5 minutes.

Once cooked, crumble the feta over the top, scatter over the fresh mint, if using, slide the frittata onto a plate and enjoy.

USE YOUR LEFTOVER …

feta:
page 76

CHICKEN + SWEETCORN SOUP

Prep Time: 5 minutes
Cook Time: 5 minutes

This soup feels slightly magical to me, in that I can't believe how quickly it comes together and how, with so few ingredients, you get such a substantial result. A salty soy-based broth with sweet bursts of corn and silky strands of egg stirred in – this is the meal to cook when you really don't feel like cooking.

300ml boiling water

1 chicken stock cube or pot

1 chicken breast, sliced into
   1cm strips

75g sweetcorn, fresh or frozen

2 tsp cornflour

2–3 tsp soy sauce

1 egg

black pepper

To serve:

1 spring onion, finely sliced

crispy chilli oil (optional)

Add the boiling water and stock cube or pot to a saucepan and bring to a gentle simmer. Add the chicken and the sweetcorn to the stock and simmer for 3 minutes – you don't want it to boil as that will toughen the chicken.

While that's simmering, add the cornflour to a bowl, then take a couple of tablespoons of the soup and add it to the cornflour. Whisk together until you have a smooth slurry. After the 3 minutes, add the slurry to the soup, along with the soy sauce and a good crack of pepper. Stir and cook for 1 minute. While that's cooking, crack the egg into the cornflour bowl and whisk until it's broken up.

Slowly pour the egg on top of the soup, let it sit for a few seconds, then stir it in. Let it cook for 1 final minute before topping with the sliced spring onion and a spoonful of chilli oil, if using.

USE YOUR LEFTOVER…
chicken breast:
page 18

CREAMY GREEN LINGUINE

Prep Time: 5 minutes
Cook Time: 15 minutes

In a way, this linguine changed my life. It was the first recipe in the series to take off on social media, bringing new people and new opportunities into my life. It's an exceptionally simple recipe that uses the same water to cook both the pasta and the vegetables, which you then use to create a velvety, carbonara-esque sauce with the cheese and egg. I've retested this and tweaked it since its original conception and, though I can't promise it will change your life, I can promise it will be delicious.

100g linguine

1 egg

45g pecorino, grated, plus extra
   to serve

½–1 tsp chilli flakes

75g broccoli, cut into small florets

handful of spinach leaves

juice of ½ large lemon

salt and black pepper

Put a pan of boiling salted water over a high heat. Add the linguine and cook for 6–7 minutes.

While this is cooking, crack the egg into a bowl and whisk with a fork. Add the cheese to the egg along with the chilli flakes and a good crack of pepper. Mix this together until combined.

Once the pasta has had 6–7 minutes, add the broccoli and the spinach to the water and cook everything for a further 3 minutes.

Take 4 tablespoons of the pasta water and add it to the egg and cheese mixture, then mix together to temper the egg and prevent it from scrambling.

When the pasta and veg are done, drain and place them back in the pan off the heat. Add the lemon juice, then the egg and cheese mixture to the pan and mix everything together. Once combined, place back on a medium-low heat until the sauce has thickened, is silky and coats the pasta.

Serve with a final crack of pepper and a little extra cheese.

USE YOUR LEFTOVER:

broccoli:
page 22

GYOZA STIR FRY

Prep Time: 10 minutes
Cook Time: 10 minutes

I love having a bag of frozen gyoza in the freezer for an undemanding lunch, dinner or side dish. In this stir-fry they sort of take the place of both meat and noodle, combining the two into chewy, slightly crispy parcels, though of course you could add both meat and/or noodles as well. As with most stir-fries, this is versatile, so use any flavour of gyoza and feel free to switch up the vegetables as you like.

1 tbsp vegetable oil
4–6 frozen gyoza
75g broccoli, cut into florets
½ red pepper, finely sliced
½ white onion, finely sliced
1 spring onion, cut into 2.5cm pieces
2 garlic cloves, thinly sliced

For the sauce:
1 tbsp soy sauce
2 tsp oyster sauce
2 tsp honey
juice of ½ lime

To serve:
2–3 tbsp roasted salted peanuts,
    roughly chopped

Place a large frying pan over a high heat. Add the oil and place the gyoza in the pan. Add a splash of water, then place a lid on and let the gyoza fry and steam for 5 minutes.

After 5 minutes, add the vegetables and garlic to the pan and fry for 3 minutes.

After 3 minutes, add all the ingredients for the sauce to the pan. Toss together and cook for a final 2 minutes, then serve up and sprinkle over the peanuts.

USE YOUR LEFTOVER
red pepper and
onion:
page 21

SMASH BURGER FLATBREAD

Testing and developing myriad versions of multiple recipes in a single day often means taking bites of every meal, but never really sitting down to eat the whole thing. This was absolutely not the case with this smash burger flatbread. I took my usual bite, then I took another, and then I pulled out my chair and devoured the entire thing, juice and sauce dripping down my hands. Thank goodness I was alone. Ridiculously quick and unfathomably delicious, this is so much more than the sum of its parts.

Prep Time: 5 minutes
Cook Time: 5 minutes

Place the flatbread on your chopping board. Lay half of the cheese on top of the flatbread, then take the mince and press it onto the flatbread, on top of the cheese, in an even layer. Season the beef well with salt and pepper.

Heat a frying pan over a high heat and add a little olive oil. Once hot, carefully place your flatbread in the pan, beef side down. Cook on this side for 2 minutes or until the bottom is nicely browned and slightly crisp.

Drizzle a little oil over the flatbread, then flip the whole thing over. Place the rest of the cheese on top of the beef (that's now facing up), then cook for a further 2 minutes with a lid on the pan so the flatbread gets crisp and the cheese melts. If your pan doesn't have a lid, you can use a plate.

Once the flatbread is crisp and the cheese has melted, take the flatbread out of the pan and place on your serving plate. Top with your lettuce, tomato, pickles and red onion, if using, and whichever sauces you like.

1 Greek-style flatbread
40g your favourite cheese, sliced
125g beef mince
extra virgin olive oil
salt and black pepper

For the toppings:
lettuce, thinly sliced
tomato, thinly sliced
pickles, thinly sliced
red onion, thinly sliced (optional)
sauces of your choice: ketchup, mayo, American mustard

USE YOUR LEFTOVER

beef mince: page 26

LOADED JACKET POTATO

Prep Time: 10 minutes
Cook Time: 25 minutes

If a jacket potato with beans and a plate of loaded nachos started a family this would be their firstborn. Piled up with saucy beans, melty cheese and crispy chorizo and topped with hot jalapeños and cooling sour cream, we've levelled up the average jacket. If you don't love beans, you could do this without and the result would be something akin to a loaded potato skin, which is no bad thing.

1 baking potato
extra virgin olive oil
200g baked beans
30–40g Cheddar
    or Red Leicester, grated
2 tbsp jarred jalapeños, drained,
    half finely chopped, half sliced
30g chorizo, cut into ½cm cubes
3 tbsp sour cream
salt

Preheat the oven to 220°C (200°C fan).

Microwave the potato for 8–12 minutes, depending on its size. You want it to be just cooked through. (If you don't have a microwave, you can bake it in the oven for 45–60 minutes).

Once cooked, place the potato in a small ovenproof frying pan or baking dish and cut a cross in it. Push out the four quarters of the potato, then drizzle over a little olive oil and season with salt. Spoon over the baked beans, then sprinkle the cheese over the beans. Scatter over the chopped jalapeños and the chorizo, then bake in the oven for 15 minutes or until the cheese has melted and the chorizo and potato are slightly crisp.

Spoon over the sour cream, then sprinkle over the remaining sliced jalapeños and serve.

USE YOUR LEFTOVER:
sour cream:
page 141

KALE, SALMON + SWEET POTATO SALAD WITH A CREAMY GARLIC DRESSING

Prep Time: 10 minutes
Cook Time: 30 minutes

I was a kale denier for many years as I often find it tough, fibrous and bland. This still can be the case if it's not prepared properly, but here the kale is roasted, which softens its fibrous nature and crisps its frilly edges and, when coated in this creamy garlic dressing, actually transforms it into a lovely salad. Roasted sweet potato in a salad adds bulk and substance but also a lovely softness, though you could definitely replace this with squash or white potato, if you prefer.

1 sweet potato (200–300g),
    cut into 2.5cm cubes
extra virgin olive oil
100g kale
1 salmon fillet
½ avocado, chopped into cubes
salt and black pepper

For the dressing:
3 tbsp natural yoghurt
1 tbsp mayonnaise
1 tsp honey
½ tsp Dijon mustard
juice of ½ lemon
1 garlic clove, grated

Preheat the oven to 220°C (200°C fan).

Place the sweet potato pieces on a baking tray, drizzle with olive oil and season well with salt and pepper. Roast for 20 minutes.

Meanwhile, prepare the dressing in your serving bowl (you want to use quite a large bowl). Add the yoghurt, mayonnaise, honey and mustard to the bowl, along with the lemon juice and garlic. Mix everything together until well combined.

Once the potato has had 20 minutes, take it out and add the kale and the salmon to the tray. Drizzle both with olive oil and season with salt and pepper. Use your hands or tongs to toss the kale, squeezing it to soften it slightly as you do. Place back in the oven and roast for a further 10 minutes.

Once everything is cooked, add the sweet potato and kale to the bowl of dressing. Add the avocado and toss everything together until coated in the dressing. Remove the skin and flake the salmon over the top of the salad in small pieces before serving.

USE YOUR LEFTOVER…
salmon fillet:
page 70

CROQUE MADAME PASTRY

Prep Time: 15 minutes
Cook Time: 25 minutes

It's a Sunday morning, you've had a lie-in, you're still in your pyjamas, cup of tea in hand and this croque madame pastry is in the oven. It's going to be a good day! I adore this recipe, and almost always favour savoury pastries over sweet ones. The nutmeg and mustard are heroes here, bringing another layer of flavour to the plate and cutting through the cheese. You could leave off the egg, like a croque monsieur, or leave out the ham if you want to keep it vegetarian.

100g ready-rolled puff pastry
30g cream cheese
¼–½ tsp Dijon mustard
pinch of grated nutmeg
1–2 slices of ham
30g Cheddar, grated
1 egg
salt and black pepper

Preheat the oven to 180°C (160°C fan). Line a small baking tray with baking paper.

Unroll the pastry onto the lined baking tray and cut off a 12 x 20cm rectangle. Score a border in the pastry around 1cm in from the edge.

Spoon the cream cheese and Dijon mustard onto the pastry, then use the back of a spoon to spread this out to the edges of the border. Sprinkle or grate over the nutmeg.

Lay the ham over the cream cheese, then sprinkle over the Cheddar, leaving a small gap in the middle of the pastry where the egg will sit.

Bake for 20 minutes, then take out of the oven and crack the egg into the centre. Season with salt and pepper, then bake for another 5–10 minutes until the egg is cooked to your liking.

USE YOUR LEFTOVER…
puff pastry:
page 212

GNOCCHI CON TOMATE

If you're going to make one recipe from this book, make it this one! Well, actually, make them all, but definitely include this one. It. Is. Divine. It may seem simple, and it most definitely is, but it is mighty. The crisp bounce of the gnocchi replaces the bread traditionally used in Spanish 'pan con tomate' and takes it from a light lunch to a more substantial meal. Good-quality tomatoes are essential here, as well as generous seasoning, as that's where most of the flavour comes from.

Prep Time: 10 minutes
Cook Time: 5 minutes

Start by grating your tomatoes onto your serving bowl or plate. Use the large hole of the grater and grate until you are left with the skin of the tomato, which you can discard. Add the garlic to the tomato and mix together. Season with flaky salt and a good drizzle of olive oil.

Heat a frying pan over a medium-high heat and add another good drizzle of olive oil to the pan. Add in the gnocchi and fry for 4–5 minutes until golden and crispy. Season with salt, then spoon over the tomato mixture.

Scatter the basil leaves over the top before serving.

2 good-quality large vine tomatoes
1 garlic clove, grated
extra virgin olive oil
150g gnocchi
5g fresh basil leaves, torn if large
flaky sea salt

USE YOUR LEFTOVER...

gnocchi:
page 67

TORTELLINI + SAUSAGE SOUP

Prep Time: 10 minutes
Cook Time: 20 minutes

A hearty, satisfying bowl, this soup is another great recipe to use up leftovers. It's perfect with scraggly sausage bits, but you could easily replace them with spare mince or meatballs. Similarly, if you have gnocchi leftover from another recipe, you could use that instead of the tortellini, and any leafy greens would work well in place of the spinach.

extra virgin olive oil
½ white onion, finely diced
½ carrot, finely diced
2 sausages (or use 100–125g
   mince or meatballs)
1 garlic clove, thinly sliced
1 tbsp tomato purée
300ml water
½ chicken or vegetable stock
   cube or pot
100g fresh tortellini or gnocchi
handful of spinach leaves or roughly
   chopped kale
salt and black pepper

Heat the olive oil in a saucepan over a medium heat. Sauté the onion and carrot for 7–8 minutes or until soft.

Break the sausage into small crumbles, then add to the pan, along with the garlic, and cook for another 3–4 minutes until browned. Season with salt and pepper.

Add the tomato purée and cook for 2 minutes before adding in the water and stock cube or pot. Bring to a gentle boil, then add in the tortellini or gnocchi and the greens and cook for 3–4 minutes until the pasta/gnocchi is cooked.

USE YOUR LEFTOVER ...

sausages:
page 16

FISH FINGER SANDWICH WITH CRISPY CAPERS

Prep Time: 5 minutes
Cook Time: 15 minutes

I'm sure we can all agree on the superiority of a fish finger sandwich – up there with the best of the sandwiches, and surely the best way to eat fish fingers. My dad used to eat them for breakfast before a school exam, a tradition that my siblings and I happily carried on all throughout our schooling. I entirely appreciate the unembellished beauty of fish fingers squished between slices of cheap, white bread lathered in butter but, in case you're feeling fancy, I've developed a version with crusty baguette stuffed with a lemony mayonnaise, pickles and crispy capers that have been baked with the fish fingers. A fine sandwich if ever I saw one.

3–4 fish fingers
2 tbsp capers
extra virgin olive oil
½ par-baked baguette

To serve:
mayonnaise
juice of ½ lemon
romaine lettuce leaves
sliced pickles
salt

Preheat the oven to 230°C (210°C fan).

Place the fish fingers on a lined baking tray. Spoon your capers onto a piece of kitchen roll and gently pat them dry to remove any excess liquid. Add these to the baking tray next to the fish fingers and drizzle over a little olive oil. Bake for 5 minutes, then add the baguette to the tray and bake for another 7–8 minutes until the fish fingers and baguette are cooked, and the capers are crispy.

Assemble your sandwich by slicing the baguette in half and spreading over a generous dollop of mayonnaise. Squeeze over the lemon juice and mix that together with the mayonnaise. Add a few leaves of lettuce, then place the fish fingers on top. Add slices of pickle, then top with the crispy capers, a sprinkle of salt and the top half of the baguette, and tuck in

USE YOUR LEFTOVER...

capers:
page 81

CREAMY SCRAMBLED EGGS WITH COTTAGE CHEESE

Prep Time: 5 minutes
Cook Time: 5 minutes

I'd be enormously surprised if I were the first person to introduce you to scrambled, or even cheesy scrambled eggs, but you may not have had them with cottage cheese before. I love it because it makes the eggs extra creamy and simultaneously gives a tang that cuts through the richness of the buttery eggs. Topped with spicy chilli oil and the bite of a spring onion, this is a great way to change up a classic.

2 eggs
knob of butter
slice of bread
3 tbsp cottage cheese
salt and black pepper

To serve:
1 spring onion, finely sliced
crispy chilli oil

Add the eggs and butter to a cold saucepan and whisk thoroughly until the egg whites and egg yolks are fully mixed together.

Put your bread on to toast, then place the eggs over a low heat and use a spatula to gently stir them until they are scrambled but still creamy.

Add in the cottage cheese and season with salt and pepper. Stir the mixture together and cook for another minute before spooning over your toast.

Sprinkle the spring onion over the top and spoon over some chilli oil to serve.

USE YOUR LEFTOVER... eggs: page 102

CHEESY GOCHUJANG NOODLES

Prep Time: 5 minutes
Cook Time: 10 minutes

It took me far too many years to try instant noodles (we're talking 25+ years…) but now there's almost always a packet in my cupboard, just in case. Whether you're needing to nurse a hangover, or settling in for a night on the sofa, you can't go too far wrong with a packet of instant noodles and a kettle. I've jazzed them up slightly here, adding spicy Korean gochujang paste, a generous amount of cheese and fresh spring onions. Choose any flavour noodle you like, or you could use straight-to-wok noodles for this too, in which case you may need to use less water.

1 tbsp sesame oil
2 garlic cloves, finely diced
1 tbsp gochujang paste
250ml boiling water
1 packet of instant noodles
70g mozzarella, grated
soy sauce (optional)

To serve:
1 spring onion, thinly sliced
   at an angle
sesame seeds
fresh coriander (optional)

Heat a saucepan over a medium heat, add the sesame oil and sauté the garlic for 2–3 minutes. Add in the gochujang and cook for another minute or two. Add in the water and stir together.

Add in your noodles, along with any flavour packets that come with the noodles, and cook for 3–5 minutes until the noodles are soft. Add in the mozzarella and mix everything together until the cheese has melted. Loosen with a splash of water if needed. Taste, and season with soy sauce, if you like.

Serve up the noodles topped with the spring onion, a sprinkle of sesame seeds and fresh coriander, if you like.

USE YOUR LEFTOVER…

gochujang paste:
page 86

HASH BROWN BREAKFAST SKILLET

If there's one thing that can make a hash brown (which is already an almost perfect food product) better, it's cheese. And if you're going to go to the effort of making yourself breakfast you might as well make it this recipe, because it has every component of an excellent brekkie except bacon, though you could easily add that when you bake the hash browns. Now there's an idea... If you start seeing this on the brunch menu of every overpriced restaurant in London, you'll know who to credit.

Prep Time: 5 minutes
Cook Time: 30 minutes

Preheat the oven to 200°C (180°C fan).

Add a little olive oil to a small ovenproof frying pan or baking dish and add the hash browns. Bake in the oven for 20 minutes.

Take the pan/dish out of the oven and sprinkle over the cheese. Crack the egg into the middle of the hash browns and season with salt and pepper. Bake for another 5–10 minutes until the egg is cooked to your liking.

Top with a spoonful of crispy chilli oil, the sliced avocado, coriander and the lime juice.

extra virgin olive oil
4 frozen hash browns
30g Cheddar or mozzarella, grated
1 egg
salt and black pepper

To serve:
crispy chilli oil
½ avocado, sliced
small handful of fresh
   coriander, shredded
juice of ¼ lime

USE YOUR LEFTOVER...
avocado:
page 114

CHICKPEA, TURMERIC + COCONUT CURRY

Prep Time: 5 minutes
Cook Time: 20 minutes

This curry uses exceptionally minimal fresh produce, relying instead on tins and store-cupboard ingredients. Turmeric is one of my favourite spices and I love its prominent flavour in this curry. If I were you, I would forgo any cutlery here and instead tear off soft hunks of naan or flatbread to use as your spoon.

extra virgin olive oil
½ white onion, finely diced
2 garlic cloves, finely diced
1 tsp ground turmeric
½ tsp garam masala
½ tsp mild curry powder
⅓ tin chickpeas
    (120g drained weight)
200ml coconut milk
½ vegetable stock pot

To serve:
fresh coriander, finely chopped
naan or flatbread

Add a little olive oil to a saucepan over a medium heat. Fry the onion for a couple of minutes before adding in the garlic and sautéing for a couple more minutes. Add in the spices and cook for 2 minutes until fragrant.

Add in the chickpeas, coconut milk, stock pot and a splash of water and let this simmer away for 10–15 minutes until the curry has thickened.

Serve topped with the coriander, alongside a bread of your choice and an extra drizzle of coconut milk, if you like.

USE YOUR LEFTOVER

chickpeas:
page 100

PRAWN + CHORIZO PIL PIL

Prep Time: 10 minutes
Cook Time: 10 minutes

We're playing with a classic Spanish tapas dish here, Gambas Pil Pil, a simple pot of juicy fresh prawns and spiced herbs bathed in plenty of good quality olive oil. 'Pil Pil' refers to a Spanish/Basque sauce made from olive oil, garlic and chilli, which is the foundation of this dish. Chorizo adds the smoky flavours of paprika that you normally find in a Pil Pil, and the hit of fresh lemon and parsley at the end bring it all to life. Hunks of crusty bread are essential for this one.

60g chorizo, thinly sliced
3–4 tbsp extra virgin olive oil
100–165g raw prawns
3–4 garlic cloves, finely chopped
1 red chilli, fincly chopped
juice of ½ lemon
5g fresh parsley, finely chopped
salt and black pepper

To serve:
crusty bread

Add the chorizo to a cold frying pan and place over a medium-high heat. Let that cook for 2–3 minutes until it has started to crisp up and release its oil.

Add the olive oil to the pan and let that heat up with the chorizo. When hot, add in the prawns, garlic and chilli and season with salt and pepper. Let that sizzle away for another 2–3 minutes until the prawns are fully cooked.

Take the pan off the heat, squeeze over the lemon juice and sprinkle over the fresh parsley. Serve with crusty bread to mop up the oil.

USE YOUR LEFTOVER …
prawns:
page 172

MARMALADE SAUSAGE TRAYBAKE

Prep Time: 15 minutes
Cook Time: 60 minutes

The first ever One Pot, One Portion recipe, this traybake will always hold a special place in my heart. It takes slightly more cooking time than other recipes in this chapter but, other than chopping some vegetables, this extra time is entirely hands-off oven time. The vegetables are interchangeable and can be adapted according to preference or leftovers and you could easily make this vegetarian or vegan by using a non-meat sausage.

150g new potatoes, cut into
   1cm cubes
extra virgin olive oil
½ leek, sliced into 1cm rings
½ red pepper, diced
100g cherry tomatoes, cut in half
2 garlic cloves, finely chopped
2–3 sausages
2 tbsp marmalade
1 tbsp wholegrain mustard
salt and black pepper

To serve:
chilli flakes (optional)

Preheat the oven to 220°C (200°C fan).

Add the potatoes to an ovenproof dish or baking tray with a little salt and olive oil and roast for 15–30 minutes until mostly soft.

Add the leek, red pepper, tomatoes and garlic, then place the sausages on top of the vegetables and drizzle everything with olive oil. Spoon over the marmalade and the mustard and season with salt and pepper. Mix everything together, then bake for 30 minutes or until the sausages and potatoes are fully cooked.

Serve sprinkled with chilli flakes, if you like.

USE YOUR LEFTOVER

sausages:
page 120

This chapter is here to encourage you to invest in yourself and to show yourself a little extra love. Recipes that feel luxurious, for when you want to carve out a bit of extra time in the day to cook, or to use ingredients that you wouldn't normally reach for (and might have a higher price tag). From the ultimate Friday night steak and crisp sandwich with chimichurri, to salami and hot honey frying pan pizza and not one, but two roast dinners. Treat yourself to something extra special.

SPECIAL

STEAK + CRISP SANDWICH WITH CHIMICHURRI

Prep Time: 15 minutes
Cook Time: 10 minutes

This sandwich transcends the two ends of the eating-on-your-own spectrum. At one end, we have the humble crisp sandwich – the meal you eat when no one else is around and quite frankly you can't be arsed. And at the other end, a perfectly cooked steak, a date night for one, a weekend treat. Together they create MAGIC. Salt and vinegar crisps would be my choice, but other flavours are available, of course.

1 steak (fillet or rib eye)
extra virgin olive oil
knob of butter
1 large ciabatta roll
handful of rocket leaves
1 packet of thick/crinkle-cut salt
   and vinegar crisps
salt and black pepper

For the chimichurri:
5g fresh coriander, finely chopped
5g fresh parsley, finely chopped
1 small garlic clove, finely chopped
½ red chilli, finely chopped
1½ tbsp extra virgin olive oil
2 tsp red wine vinegar
pinch of sugar

Take the steak out of the fridge to rest at room temperature while you make your chimichurri.

Add the herbs, garlic and chilli to a bowl along with the oil and vinegar. Season with a pinch of salt and sugar.

Heat a frying pan over a high heat. While that gets hot, put your steak on your chopping board and drizzle with a little olive oil, covering both sides. Season generously with salt and pepper. When the pan is very hot, add the steak and allow it to cook on both sides until it is done to your liking. For a rare fillet steak, I cook it for 90 seconds on each side. When cooked, let it rest on the chopping board and add a knob of butter to the pan. Slice your ciabatta in half and place it cut-side down in the butter to toast.

When the ciabatta is golden brown and toasted, you can start assembling the sandwich. Place the rocket on top of the bottom half of the ciabatta. Slice the steak into 1–2cm slices and lay it on top of the rocket. Spoon over the chimichurri. Finally, lay the crisps on top of the steak and sauce and top with the other half of the ciabatta. Devour.

USE YOUR LEFTOVER:
steak:
page 21

TUNA TOSTADAS WITH AVOCADO, JALAPEÑOS + PICKLED GINGER

This feels like a fusion between crispy tacos and a spicy tuna roll, brought alive by the bright, fresh flavours of pickled ginger and jalapeños. We're using fresh tuna steaks for these tostadas, which are lightly seared in sesame oil to give a subtle, toasted flavour while retaining a pink blush. Fresh sour cream and avocado contrast with the crunch of the tostada for an explosion of texture and flavour.

Prep Time: 10 minutes
Cook Time: 10 minutes

Add enough sesame oil to a frying pan so that the bottom of the pan is covered with a shallow layer. Heat over a medium-high heat. Meanwhile, grab a couple of pieces of kitchen roll and place them on your serving plate or chopping board.

Once hot, fry your tortillas for 1–2 minutes on each side until golden brown. Once golden, place them on the kitchen roll to allow excess oil to drain off. Each will crisp up as it cools down.

Turn the heat down slightly and season the tuna steak generously with salt on both sides. Fry in the oil for 1–2 minutes on each side (this will depend on how rare you want your steak to be and how thick your steak is – 90 seconds on each side is a good place to start if you are unsure). Once fried, place this on the kitchen roll too. Allow to cool slightly.

Place 1 tablespoon of sour cream on each tortilla. Evenly distribute the avocado slices on top of the sour cream, then squeeze over the lime juice and season each tortilla with a generous pinch of salt. Lay the jalapeños on top of the avocado.

Slice your tuna steak into 8 slices, against the grain if possible, then lay the slices on top of the jalapeños on each tortilla. Finish with 1 teaspoon of pickled ginger on top of each tortilla and a twist of pepper.

3–5 tbsp sesame oil
2 small flour tortillas
1 tuna steak
2 tbsp sour cream
½ avocado, thinly sliced
juice of ¼ lime
2 tbsp jarred or fresh jalapeños, sliced
2 tsp pickled ginger, drained
salt and black pepper

USE YOUR LEFTOVER...
tortilla wraps:
page 76

MORTADELLA + MOZZARELLA FOCACCIA

Prep Time: 110 minutes
Cook Time: 30 minutes

Don't get me wrong, eating an entire loaf of bread yourself can be a transcendent experience, but large loaves don't always suit the solo diner. With bread being one of the most frequently wasted food items, sometimes a single serving is just what you need and that's exactly what we've got here. I've filled this freshly baked focaccia with mozzarella and mortadella for an Italian-inspired feast, but the possibilities for this miniature loaf are endless; top or fill with anything your heart desires.

For the focaccia:
150g strong white bread flour
½ tsp fast-action dried yeast
½ tsp caster sugar
½ tsp flaky sea salt, plus
    extra for sprinkling
150ml warm water
1 tsp extra virgin olive oil,
    plus extra for drizzling
handful of pitted olives

For the sandwich:
1 tbsp fresh pesto
3–4 slices of mortadella
70g fresh mozzarella, drained
    and sliced
handful of rocket leaves
drizzle of balsamic vinegar

Add the flour, yeast, sugar and salt to a bowl and mix together. Add the water and oil and mix together until combined and you have a mostly smooth, but wet dough (don't be alarmed at how wet it is, this is what gives it a lovely texture and those bigger air bubbles). You can oil your hands to make mixing easier or use a rubber spatula.

Take a small pie dish or ovenproof frying pan and line it with baking paper. Drizzle with olive oil, then place the dough into the dish/pan. Drizzle a little more oil over the top, then smooth down and press out with your fingers, making little dimples in it as you go. Leave this to rise in a warm place for 60 minutes. Then, using your fingers, again press into the dough to create little dimples and push the olives into the dough. Leave to rise for a final 30 minutes.

Preheat the oven to 200°C (180°C fan). Once risen, sprinkle with a little extra flaky salt and bake for 25–30 minutes or until golden brown. Leave to cool before cutting in half horizontally.

Once cooled, assemble the sandwich. Spread the pesto over the bottom half of the focaccia, then lay over the mortadella and the mozzarella slices. Season with a little salt, then top with the rocket. Drizzle over some balsamic vinegar, then top with the other half of the focaccia.

USE YOUR LEFTOVER

mozzarella:
page 51

LOBSTER SPAGHETTI WITH LEMON + TOMATOES

Prep Time: 15 minutes
Cook Time: 15 minutes

Although lobster is typically the most expensive item on a menu, cooking it at home means you get the same lobster luxury at a slightly more accessible price point. Don't get me wrong, this still feels like a treat but it's the perfect dish for a date night for one. Cooking lobster can feel intimidating, but I think you'll be surprised by how simple it is to cook – this whole dish comes together in around 30 minutes.

100g of lobster meat (approximately
   2 small lobster tails)
100g spaghetti
125g cherry tomatoes
juice of 1 lemon
3 tbsp double cream
10g fresh basil or parsley,
   finely chopped
½ tsp chilli flakes
15g Parmesan, grated
salt and black pepper

USE YOUR LEFTOVER ...

double cream:
page 163

Place a pan of salted water over a medium-high heat. Prep the lobster tails by taking a pair of scissors and cutting the top of the shell down the middle lengthways from the edge of the tail to the end. This makes them cook more evenly and makes it slightly easier to cut them open after. Place the lobster tails in the water and boil for 2½–3 minutes.

Use a pair of tongs to take the lobster tails out of the water and place them on your chopping board. Skim any froth off the top of the water, then place back on the heat and add in the spaghetti. Boil for 6 minutes. Meanwhile, take your tomatoes and make a small cut in their skin (this will help them soften later).

Next, prep the cooked lobster. Take a sharp knife and cut down through the shell, along the cut that you made before boiling, to split the tails in half. Using a spoon, scoop out the lobster meat and dispose of the shells (or save for a fish stock). Roughly chop the meat into 2–3cm pieces – I like to keep them quite big so you get a nice meaty bite of lobster when you eat it.

After the pasta has been boiling for 6 minutes, add in the tomatoes and cook for another 3–4 minutes until the pasta is almost done but not quite.

Drain the pasta and tomatoes, keeping a little cooking water in the pan, then add back to the pan and turn the heat to low. Add the lobster, the lemon juice, cream, most of the herbs and the chilli flakes and use the tongs to stir everything together. Add the grated Parmesan and stir again. As you stir, the tomatoes should break down slightly and the sauce should become silky and creamy.

Taste and season with salt and pepper, then serve with a final sprinkle of the remaining herbs and an extra wedge of lemon.

TRUFFLED MUSHROOM PAPPARDELLE

For the most part, I despise mushrooms and for a while I was adamant that they would find no place in this book. However, as Rory O'Connell said in class one day at Ballymaloe, 'it's good to know that you are wrong sometimes, otherwise one could become unbearable,' and I'm glad to say I was wrong (and thus, hopefully remain bearable... for now). Mushrooms do deserve their place in this book and this creamy, truffled pappardelle is that place. You can choose how truffle-y you want this pasta to be or, if you're not a fan at all, you could substitute with a really good olive oil instead.

Prep Time: 5 minutes
Cook Time: 15 minutes

Add a good drizzle of truffle oil to a large frying pan over a medium-high heat. Sauté the mushrooms for 4–5 minutes until deep golden brown. Once the mushrooms are done, add the garlic to the pan and cook for another minute or two.

Add in the mascarpone and the water. Stir together until smooth, then add in the fresh pappardelle and cook for 5–6 minutes or until the pasta is just al dente, stirring frequently. Add more water if needed to create a loose, glossy sauce.

Add the Parmesan and parsley to the pasta once it's almost cooked. Stir everything together and season with salt and pepper.

Serve with a final drizzle of truffle oil.

good drizzle of truffle oil

100g button or chestnut mushrooms, thinly sliced

2 garlic cloves, finely chopped

3 tbsp mascarpone

200ml water

150g fresh pappardelle

20g Parmesan, grated

5g fresh parsley, finely chopped

salt and black pepper

USE YOUR LEFTOVER...

mascarpone:
page 26

CHICKEN OR PANEER BIRYANI

Prep Time: 5 minutes
Cook Time: 50 minutes

A dish perfected over years across the subcontinent and South Asia, steeped in both history and culture, this is my one-pot, one-portion version of a biryani. Traditionally an intricate dish using layers of rice and meat, accompanied by an eclectic mix of herbs and a medley of spices, as well as various garnishes. The aim here was simplicity while still getting that *mazedar* (delicious) flavour!

1 tbsp ghee or vegetable oil
½ white onion, finely diced
½ cinnamon stick
4 cardamom pods, lightly crushed
1 star anise
3 cloves
2 garlic cloves, grated
10g fresh ginger, grated
1 skinless, boneless chicken thigh, or
    100g paneer, cut into 2cm cubes
½ tsp ground turmeric
1 tsp garam masala
1 bay leaf
3 tbsp natural yoghurt, plus
    extra to serve
125ml boiling water
½ chicken stock pot
small pinch of saffron
85g basmati rice, rinsed
salt and black pepper

To serve:
fresh coriander, finely chopped
crispy onions (shop-bought)

Heat the ghee or oil in a small frying pan. Once melted, add in the onion and a little salt and cook over a low heat for around 15 minutes. You want it to soften and turn a golden brown from a longer cooking time, as opposed to a higher heat.

Once the onion is soft and golden, add in the cinnamon stick, cardamom, star anise and cloves and cook for 2–3 minutes. Next, add in the garlic, ginger and chicken/paneer and fry for 2–3 minutes. Once the chicken is sealed, add in the turmeric, garam masala, bay leaf and yoghurt. Season with salt again, and a good crack of pepper, then stir together and cook for a minute or two.

Turn the heat to low, then add the boiling water to a jug along with the chicken stock pot and the saffron, and mix together. Spoon the rinsed rice on top of the chicken/paneer in the pan in an even layer. Gently pour over the stock and saffron water, then place a lid or a tight cover of tin foil on the pan and cook for 15 minutes, ensuring the heat is very low.

After 15 minutes, check the rice, it should be still a little undercooked and there should be some moisture in the pan. If the rice is looking very dry, add a small splash of water, then place the lid/foil back on, turn off the heat and let it steam for 10 more minutes, until the rice is fully cooked.

Once it's cooked, serve up with another spoonful of yoghurt, the coriander and some crispy onions.

USE YOUR LEFTOVER

chicken thigh:
page 82

FRENCH ONION SOUP

Prep Time: 10 minutes
Cook Time: 80 minutes

Onion soups have been popular for thousands of years and, whilst seemingly unpretentious and unassuming, they pack a huge punch of flavour. Umami-rich with sweet, caramelised onions, the method and ingredients for this soup are simple, but in order to achieve ultimate depth of flavour, you do need to set some time aside to give this soup the love it needs. I can promise this will be time well spent, though, as the gratification this comforting bowl provides is more than worth it.

30g butter
2 small white onions,
    cut into 1cm slices
75ml white wine
300ml water
½ beef stock pot
3 sprigs of fresh thyme
1 bay leaf
pinch of sugar (optional)
salt and black pepper

To serve:
crusty bread
grated Gruyère
fresh chives, finely
    chopped (optional)

Heat the butter in a saucepan and, once melted, add in the onions. Cook over a low heat, with a lid on, for 30–60 minutes, stirring frequently, until the onions are golden brown and slightly jammy.

Turn up the heat to medium and add the wine. Cook for 5 minutes or until most of the liquid has evaporated. Add in the water, beef stock pot, thyme, bay leaf and a good crack of pepper. Bring to the boil, then simmer for 10 minutes.

Taste and season with salt and a pinch of sugar, if it needs it. It should taste rich, salty and slightly sweet.

Toast your bread slightly, then begin plating up the soup. You can remove the thyme and bay, if you like, then sprinkle over some grated Gruyère, then place your toast on top and finish with a final sprinkle of Gruyère. You can let this melt with the heat of the soup, or you can place the bowl under a hot grill for a couple of minutes to melt and crisp up (ensuring the bowl is ovenproof). Sprinkle over fresh chives to serve, if you like.

USE YOUR LEFTOVER...
white wine:
page 172

SALAMI + HOT HONEY FRYING PAN PIZZA

Prep Time: 110 minutes
Cook Time: 10 minutes

With takeaways and oven-ready options galore, I can see why making your own pizza might not appeal. However, this recipe couldn't be simpler. The hands-on prep time is minimal and the pizza cooks in less time than your standard shop-bought alternative. A hot pan is key to the perfect crust, and after that, you can go wild with toppings. Here I've opted for the complementary contrast of spicy and sweet, with peppery salami and chilli-spiked honey. A fiery fusion you'll come back to again and again.

For the dough:

150g strong white bread flour

½ tsp fast-action dried yeast

½ tsp sugar

large pinch of salt

1 tbsp extra virgin olive oil, plus extra for drizzling

100ml warm water

For the topping:

4 tbsp pizza sauce or passata

7 slices of salami

80g block mozzarella (if using fresh, dry it well)

1–2 tsp honey

chilli flakes (optional)

rocket leaves

USE YOUR LEFTOVER...

passata:
page 24

Start by making the pizza dough. Add the flour, yeast, sugar, salt, olive oil and water to a bowl. Mix together with a spatula, then once everything is incorporated, knead just for a couple of minutes until the dough comes together in a ball. If it is really sticky, add a tiny bit more flour, but you don't want it to be dry at all. Lift out the dough and add a little more olive oil to the bowl. Lightly cover the dough ball in the oil, then leave in the bowl in a warm place, covered with cling film, to rise for at least 1 hour, but up to 2 hours.

Once the dough has risen, tip onto a surface, then flatten out slightly with your fingers. Shape into a round by bringing the edges of the dough into the centre. Repeat until you have a ball, then use the palms of your hands to shape until smooth and tight. Leave to rise for another 15–30 minutes. Once rested, preheat the grill to the highest temperature. Place a large cast-iron frying pan over a high heat while you make your pizza.

Drizzle a little olive oil on a clean counter, then take your pizza dough out of the bowl and, using your hands, stretch and press it into a circle, with a slightly thicker crust around the edge.

Once stretched, add a drizzle of olive oil to the pan, then press in your pizza base to flatten it – be careful, the pan will be very hot by now. Turn the heat down slightly and cook for 3 minutes while you top your pizza. Spread over the pizza sauce or passata, then top with the salami and mozzarella. Drizzle over the honey and sprinkle over some chilli flakes, if you like.

Once the pizza has had 3 minutes in the pan, place the whole pan under the grill and cook for 3–6 minutes (depending on the heat of your grill), until the crust is golden, the cheese has melted and the salami is slightly crisp. Take the pizza out and top with rocket leaves. Drizzle with a little olive oil before serving.

FRESH PICI PASTA WITH PESTO

Making fresh pasta is a labour of love and who better to show that love to, than yourself? Pici is a Tuscan pasta, hand-formed into long thick strands that retain the most satisfying chew when cooked. Rolling the pasta is slightly laborious, but I find it therapeutic in many ways, setting aside time with the sole aim of creating something special for yourself – my ideal form of self-care. Having said that, I think you'll be glad you're only having to make one portion!

Prep Time: 40 minutes
Cook Time: 5 minutes

Start by making your pesto. Add the basil leaves and pine nuts to your serving bowl. Pour in the olive oil and stir in the Parmesan cheese, mixing everything together. Taste and season with salt, if necessary.

To make the pici, tip the flour onto a chopping board or clean work surface. Make a little well in the centre, then start to pour in the water. Mix with the flour to begin making a dough, then continue to add the rest of the water, combining it until you have a ball of dough. Knead the dough for 5 minutes and it will start to become slightly softer. It shouldn't feel dry or wet, but if it does you can add a little more water or flour.

Once kneaded, cut the dough into about 20 pieces. Take one piece and roll it out with the flat of your hand until it resembles fat spaghetti, around 30cm long and slightly tapered at the ends. Repeat with all the dough pieces, sprinkling flour over each piece after it has been rolled to prevent them sticking together.

Heat a pan of water and season generously with salt. Boil the pici for 2–3 minutes until it rises to the surface of the water. Add 3 tablespoons of pasta water to the pesto in your serving bowl, then drain the pasta and add this to the pesto too, tossing to coat.

Serve with a good crack of pepper and an extra grating of Parmesan.

For the pesto:
15g fresh basil leaves, finely chopped
1 tbsp pine nuts, finely chopped
3 tbsp extra virgin olive oil
15g Parmesan, grated, plus
  extra to serve
salt and black pepper

For the pici:
150g 00 pasta flour (or strong white
  bread flour), plus extra for dusting
75ml water

USE YOUR LEFTOVER ...

basil leaves:
page 119

SPICED LAMB STEAK WITH CORIANDER + DATE CHUTNEY

Prep Time: 15 minutes
Cook Time: 15 minutes

Lamb is a naturally fatty meat and, while that can be delicious, it means I usually enjoy it most when it's slow cooked, so the fat melts into the meat, and the meat falls off the bone. However, in this recipe, we're cooking it quickly using a lamb leg steak, which is a lovely lean cut of meat that's more affordable than a loin fillet, though you could definitely use that in this recipe too. The coriander and date chutney is sweet, fresh and spicy and provides the perfect base for this recipe.

---

extra virgin olive oil

200g potatoes, cut into 2.5cm cubes

1 lamb leg steak

1 tsp garam masala

75g green beans

1 tsp ground coriander

1 tsp cumin seeds

salt and black pepper

For the chutney:

15g fresh coriander, finely chopped

2 Medjool dates, pitted and finely chopped

1–2 green chillies, deseeded and finely chopped

3 tbsp natural yoghurt

1 tsp white wine vinegar

USE YOUR LEFTOVER

dates:
page 180

Start by making your chutney. Combine the coriander and dates on your chopping board to create a chunky paste. It can be hard to mix together because the dates are sticky, so I find it easiest to run my knife back and forth through them so they chop and mix together at the same time. Add both the coriander and dates to your serving bowl or plate along with the chilli, yoghurt and vinegar. Mix everything together, then taste and season with salt. Spread over the bottom of the serving bowl or plate.

Add a good drizzle of olive oil to a frying pan and heat over a medium heat. Fry the potatoes for 5 minutes while you prepare your lamb.

Place the lamb steak on your chopping board and drizzle with a little olive oil. Season with salt and pepper and add the garam masala. Rub in the oil and spices so the steak is evenly coated.

Push the potatoes to one side of the pan, then add the lamb. Fry for 3–4 minutes on each side for medium-rare, or 5–6 minutes on each side for well-done. Continue moving the potatoes around while you're doing this.

Once the lamb is cooked, take it out of the pan and let it rest while you cook the beans. Add the green beans to the potatoes along with the ground coriander and cumin seeds and season with salt. Add a splash of water and let this cook for 4–5 minutes until the potatoes and beans are fully cooked.

Place the potatoes and beans on top of the chutney, then slice the lamb and lay this on top to serve with an extra sprinkling of coriander and green chilli.

BEEF WELLINGTON WITH ROASTED POTATOES + ONIONS

Prep Time: 25 minutes
Cook Time: 45 minutes

Beef Wellington is a showstopper on any dining table, and rightly so, but it can feel intimidating to make: fear of the unknown as you slice in, praying that the beef inside is as perfectly cooked as the outside pastry. I'm hoping to dissipate some of the fear with this recipe. As it's only one portion, there's more consistency in the cooking of the beef, ensuring the perfect pink finish. I've also created a cheat's duxelles, roasting finely chopped mushrooms in the oven, so this is an uncomplicated version of a complex classic, which I love to serve with lashings of gravy.

1 beef fillet steak
30g button or chestnut
    mushrooms, finely chopped
½ tsp dried thyme
small knob of butter
150g potatoes, cut into 1–2cm cubes
1 red onion, sliced into
    1cm semi-circles
1 garlic clove, finely chopped
    or grated
extra virgin olive oil
1 tsp Dijon mustard
2 slices of prosciutto
75–100g ready-rolled
    shortcrust pastry
salt and black pepper

USE YOUR LEFTOVER :

shortcrust
pastry:
page 45

Preheat the oven to 220°C (200°C fan). Take the steak out of the fridge to rest at room temperature.

Line a baking tray with baking paper then add the chopped mushrooms. Add the thyme and a small knob of butter, then roast in the oven for 5–10 minutes.

Once roasted, place the mushrooms on your chopping board, then place the potato cubes, onion and garlic on the baking tray, drizzle over a little olive oil and season with salt and pepper. Roast for 10 minutes while you prep the Wellington.

If your steak is around 2.5cm thick, cut the steak in half so you have two smaller chunks that, when stacked, will make one steak around 5cm thick. If your steak is already thick (5cm plus), then keep it whole. Season with salt and pepper, then rub the mustard into the steak until it's evenly coated. (If using a thinner steak, place one steak half on top of the other.) Take the two slices of prosciutto and wrap them around the steak.

Unroll the pastry and cut it into two pieces that are a few centimetres larger than your steak. Spoon half of the mushrooms onto one piece of pastry. Place the wrapped steak on top of the mushrooms, then spoon the remaining mushrooms on top of the steak. Place the other piece of pastry over the top and seal, pinching and rolling the edges together in a rope effect.

Rub a little olive oil over the pastry, sprinkle over a little salt, then cut a small hole in the top. Score lines in the pastry from the hole to the crimped edge using the blunt side of your knife, without cutting through the pastry. Bake in the oven alongside the potato and onion mixture for 15 minutes for a rare Wellington, 20 minutes for medium and 25 minutes for well-done.

CAJUN SHRIMP BOIL

Prep Time: 10 minutes
Cook Time: 40 minutes

I had my first Cajun seafood boil experience on a trip to New Orleans. This city has a distinct food culture thanks to its history and geography. Cajun cuisine is a melting pot of flavours and fusions, with influence from French, West African, Spanish and Native American cultures, and the surrounding fresh and salt water provide the foundation for the city's most famous dishes. This boil is a sample of that flavour, with a deeply rich spiced sauce, juicy cobs of corn, soft potatoes and, of course, the plump king prawns. 'Nduja paste replicates a similar flavour to the traditional andouille sausage, and really any seafood would be beautiful in this dish – lobster, crab legs, crawfish, clams – go wild. It's messy, buttery, spicy and delicious.

1 tbsp extra virgin olive oil
3 garlic cloves, finely chopped
1½ tbsp 'nduja paste
1 tbsp Cajun seasoning
600ml water
½ chicken stock pot
juice of ½ lemon
200g baby or new potatoes,
   halved if on the large side
1 corn on the cob, cut into 4
100–165g raw peeled king prawns

To serve:
a few knobs of butter
handful of fresh parsley,
   finely chopped

Heat the olive oil in a small saucepan over a medium heat. Fry the garlic for a couple of minutes, then add in the 'nduja paste and Cajun seasoning and fry for a couple more minutes. Add in the water, chicken stock pot and lemon juice, then cover with a lid, bring to the boil and boil for 10 minutes.

Once the broth has boiled for 10 minutes, add the potatoes and boil for 20 minutes with the lid on. After 20 minutes, add in the corn and boil for 5 more minutes, then drop in the prawns and cook for 3–4 minutes until they have turned pink. Add a little more water if needed, but you want to be left with a slightly thick sauce.

Spoon the shrimp boil into your serving bowl, drop a few knobs of butter over, then sprinkle over the chopped parsley.

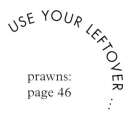

USE YOUR LEFTOVER

prawns:
page 46

BACON + POTATO GRATIN

This is not quite a tartiflette, not quite a dauphinoise, but it is quite delicious. The epitome of a winter warmer, you're practically transported to the French Alps with every mouthful. Layers of potato, smoky bacon, onion and garlic smothered in a luxurious cream sauce and topped with generous dollops of soft, ripe cheese. Green salad and pickles are an excellent accompaniment to cut through the richness... as is a glass of dry white wine.

Prep Time: 15 minutes
Cook Time: 55 minutes

Preheat the oven to 195°C (175°C fan).

Place the bacon in a small ovenproof dish and bake in the oven for 15 minutes to render slightly while you prepare the rest of your ingredients.

Once prepped, take the bacon out of the oven and spoon two-thirds of it onto your chopping board, leaving one-third in the pie dish. Lay half of the potato slices into the dish on top of the bacon, then add all the sliced onion and garlic, then another third of the bacon. Season well with salt and pepper. Layer over the other half of the potato slices and the final third of the bacon and season again with salt and pepper. Pour over the milk, followed by the cream, then break off small pieces of cheese and place evenly on the top. Finish with a final crack of pepper.

Bake for 35–40 minutes until the potatoes are soft, then let the gratin cool for a few minutes before serving with salad and pickles.

3 rashers of streaky bacon, sliced
  into thin strips
175g potatoes, cut into ½cm slices
½ small white onion, cut
  into ½cm slices
2–3 large garlic cloves, finely sliced
65ml milk
50ml double cream
50g Reblochon, Port Salut or Brie
salt and black pepper

To serve:
green salad
pickles

USE YOUR LEFTOVER...

double cream:
page 183

TUSCAN CHICKEN + POTATO

Prep Time: 10 minutes
Cook Time: 55 minutes

This dish is often referred to as 'marry me chicken' for its relationship-securing properties, but we're not thinking about anyone else when making this. This is all about you and your commitment to the most delicious dinner. I'm not sure quite how Tuscan this dish really is (probably not very), but the combination of sundried tomatoes, fresh basil and olives definitely conjures up a Mediterranean vibe.

150g new potatoes, cut
   in half if large
extra virgin olive oil
40g sundried tomatoes,
   finely chopped
2 garlic cloves, finely chopped
5–10g fresh basil, shredded
2 tsp tomato purée
40g pitted green or black olives
50ml double cream
50ml water
1 chicken breast (skin-on if possible)
handful of spinach leaves
salt and black pepper

Preheat the oven to 195°C (175°C fan).

Add the new potatoes to a small ovenproof frying pan or baking dish along with a drizzle of olive oil. Season with salt and pepper and bake in the oven for 15 minutes.

After 15 minutes, add the tomatoes, garlic, basil, tomato purée, olives, double cream and water to the pan/dish and season with salt and pepper. Mix everything together until combined, then add the chicken breast. Spoon some of the sauce on top of the chicken, then bake for 30–40 minutes until the chicken is cooked.

Once cooked, add the spinach and pop back in the oven for around 5 minutes until wilted. Mix into the sauce before serving.

USE YOUR LEFTOVER

potatoes and
chicken breast:
page 48

ROAST CHICKEN WITH SAGE, ONION + CHESTNUT STUFFING

Prep Time: 25 minutes
Cook Time: 75 minutes

I have been inundated with requests for a one-pot, one-portion roast dinner and I am thrilled to say that there is not one roast in this book, but two. That's Sundays sorted. If I had to pick just one roast to have forever, it would be a chicken roast, and this one is extra good because it's filled with sage, onion and chestnut stuffing (aka my favourite part of any roast dinner). Roasting everything in one tray means you get to make a luscious gravy out of the gubbins left in the pan, unlocking ultimate flavour.

2 tbsp vegetable or extra virgin olive oil
150–200g potatoes, peeled and cut into 5cm chunks
2 garlic cloves, peeled
1 shallot, finely chopped
1 sprig of fresh sage (about 5 leaves), finely chopped
2 tbsp chestnut purée
1 skin-on chicken breast
1 sausage, plus 1 rasher of streaky bacon (optional)
1 small carrot, cut into batons
1 parsnip, peeled and cut into batons
3 sprigs of fresh thyme
knob of butter
salt and black pepper

For the gravy:
2 tsp plain flour
½ chicken stock pot
125ml water
60g frozen peas

USE YOUR LEFTOVER ...
potatoes:
page 34

Preheat the oven to 195°C (175°C fan).

Add the oil to a large ovenproof frying pan or baking dish and add the potatoes. Keep the garlic cloves whole, but bash slightly with the flat side of your knife, then add to the pan/dish. Season lightly with salt and roast in the oven for 30 minutes.

While they are roasting, prepare the rest of the dish. Combine the shallot, sage and chestnut purée to make your stuffing. Slice a cut horizontally in the chicken breast, as if you were butterflying but without cutting all the way through, to create a little pocket. Push the stuffing into the pocket, then fold over to seal slightly. You can use cocktail sticks to keep the two sides of the chicken together if you like.

To make the pig in a blanket (if you're including it) wrap the rasher of bacon around the sausage.

Once the potatoes have had 30 minutes, take out of the oven and remove the garlic. Add the carrots, parsnips and thyme and mix together. Add the chicken and the pig in a blanket, then add a knob of butter to the top of the chicken and rub it in slightly. Season everything with salt and pepper. Roast for 30–40 minutes until the chicken is fully cooked and the vegetables are golden. Once roasted, plate up the chicken and vegetables. You can keep them in the oven (turned off) to keep warm if needed.

To make your gravy, place the pan/dish on the hob and turn the heat to medium-low. Add the flour and cook for a couple of minutes, then add the chicken stock pot and water. Whisk together until you have a smooth, thick gravy. Add the peas and cook for a couple of minutes until cooked, then serve with your roast dinner.

ROAST PORK BELLY WITH APPLE + SHALLOT GRAVY

Prep Time: 25 minutes
Cook Time: 95 minutes

Stuffing is usually my number one component of a roast dinner (see page 166) but the condiments are a close second. Fellow northerners will understand the need to have 'wet food', which is much more pleasant than it sounds, essentially just meaning a sauce or condiment with every meal. Here we have an apple and shallot gravy which is easily my favourite part – the sweet richness partners perfectly with the fatty roasted meat. Pork belly is a surprisingly affordable cut of meat to buy, but if you can only buy it in a larger chunk then you can happily portion it up and freeze it for future roasts.

200g pork belly

vegetable or extra virgin olive oil

150–200g potatoes, peeled and cut into 6cm chunks

2–3 sprigs of fresh rosemary

2 garlic cloves, peeled

1 small carrot, peeled and cut into batons

1 parsnip, peeled and cut into batons

3 small shallots, each cut into thirds

1 small apple, peeled and cut into 1cm slices

100g wedge of cabbage (Hispi is good)

1 tsp honey

1 heaped tsp wholegrain mustard

salt

For the gravy:

2 tsp plain flour

½ chicken stock pot

125ml water

USE YOUR LEFTOVER ...

vegetables:
page 98

Preheat the oven to 205°C (195°C fan).

Score the skin of the pork belly with a sharp knife and pat dry with a piece of kitchen roll. Season well with salt, then set aside. Add a good glug of oil to a baking tray and add the potatoes and rosemary on one side. Slightly crush the garlic with the flat side of your knife and add that too. Season with salt and toss in the oil. Add the pork belly to the tray and bake for 10 minutes. Turn the oven down to 185°C (165°C fan) and roast for another 20 minutes.

Add the carrot and parsnip batons to the tray next to the potatoes. On the other side of the tray, add the shallots and apple. Roast for 35 minutes, then add the cabbage to the tray with a little more oil and salt, and roast for another 15 minutes.

Spoon the honey and mustard into the carrots and parsnips and roast for a final 10 minutes.

Once cooked, plate up the pork, potatoes, carrots, parsnips and cabbage, but leave the shallots and apple in the tray. You can keep them in the oven (turned off) to stay warm if needed.

To make the gravy, place the baking tray on the hob and turn the heat to medium-low. Add the flour and cook for a couple of minutes, then add the chicken stock pot and water. Whisk together with the shallots and apple until you have a smooth, thick gravy. Serve with your roast dinner.

PORK + KIMCHI STEAMED BUNS

They may seem demanding but making fluffy steamed buns is much simpler than their appearance may convey. An uncomplicated 3-ingredient dough recipe comes together in less than 10 minutes, and the filling utilises the natural flavour of sausages and kimchi to pack a punch. Once steamed, finish with soy sauce, spicy chilli oil, fresh herbs and spring onions and you're in heaven. This makes 2 buns and, while they are quite large, I would also understand if you wanted to double up the recipe for a very hungry day.

Prep Time: 45 minutes
Cook Time: 15 minutes

Pour the flour onto a clean work surface and mix in the yeast. Create a well in the centre and slowly add the milk, bringing it together with the flour until you have a ball of dough. Knead for around 5 minutes until quite smooth and soft (it shouldn't be sticky, but you can add an extra drop of milk if needed to get a smooth consistency). Cover with a piece of damp kitchen roll and leave to rest for around 30 minutes while you prep the filling.

Take the sausage meat out of the casing and place on a chopping board. Add the ginger, kimchi and honey. Chop everything together until you have a chunky paste and season with salt and pepper.

Once the dough has rested, split it in half and roll each half into a circle around 15cm in diameter. Take half of the sausage mixture and place in the centre of one dough circle. Start pleating the edges of the dough by holding the dough between your thumb and forefinger, with your thumb in the centre, bringing in the sides of the dough around your thumb, folding it over the last piece every time to create a pleat. You should end up with a pleated dumpling with a hole in the middle where your thumb was. Repeat with the other circle of dough.

Place the dumplings in a steamer set over a pan of simmering water, put the lid on and steam the dumplings for 15 minutes.

Sprinkle over the spring onion, herbs and sesame seeds, if using, before serving with soy sauce and/or crispy chilli oil, if you like.

For the buns:
80g plain flour
¼ tsp fast-action dried yeast
40ml milk

For the filling:
1 pork sausage
5g fresh ginger, grated
40g kimchi
1 tsp honey
salt and black pepper

To serve (optional):
1 spring onion, sliced at an angle
fresh chives and/or coriander
sesame seeds
soy sauce
crispy chilli oil

USE YOUR LEFTOVER...
sausages:
page 16

CHICKEN + PRAWN PAELLA

Prep Time: 10 minutes
Cook Time: 45 minutes

A dish with so many variations can feel intimidating to try but I'm hoping to demystify paella with this recipe, its classic ingredients and clear method. Though it might be easier to make than at first imagined, the result has the taste and feel of an extra special evening meal. You could happily add other seafood too – mussels, clams or squid would be delicious – but I've kept things accessible with prawns as they're easy to find, though I do recommend buying the plumpest, juiciest prawns possible. A final flourish of lemon and fresh parsley brings this rice dish to life.

1 tbsp extra virgin olive oil
½ white onion, finely diced
½ red pepper, finely diced
1 skinless, boneless chicken thigh
    (or see method for how to remove)
2 garlic cloves, finely chopped
1 tsp paprika
75g paella rice
50ml white wine
1 large vine tomato, finely chopped
½ chicken stock cube
175ml water
80g raw peeled prawns
5g fresh parsley, finely chopped
juice of ½ lemon, plus
    a wedge to serve
salt and black pepper

USE YOUR LEFTOVER...
chicken thigh:
page 148

Heat the oil in a small frying pan over a medium-low heat. Add the onion and red pepper plus a little salt and fry for around 10 minutes until golden and soft.

If you need to remove the skin and the bone from the chicken then, using your hands and a knife to help where needed, gently pull the skin off the thigh. To remove the bone, simply cut around, keeping your knife as close to the bone as possible. Don't worry if you cut through the meat, you're going to be cutting up the thigh anyway. Once the bone has been removed, cut the chicken into 2.5cm pieces.

Once the onion and pepper are golden, add the garlic and paprika and fry for 2 minutes. Add the rice and let that toast for a couple of minutes, then deglaze the pan with the white wine. Let this cook until almost all of the liquid has been absorbed, then add the tomato, chicken, stock cube and water. Season with salt and pepper. Mix this together, then let this simmer away for around 25 minutes. You only need to stir this a couple of times. If needed, you can add an extra 50ml of water after 25 minutes if the liquid has been absorbed and the rice isn't quite cooked.

Add the prawns, stir them through and let them cook for 3–5 minutes until pink and cooked through. Taste and season with salt if needed.

Add the parsley and lemon juice and stir through before serving. Serve with a wedge of lemon.

SPICED LAMB + AUBERGINE WITH PITTA

Prep Time: 15 minutes
Cook Time: 20 minutes

This recipe is based on the Middle Eastern dish, fatteh, which is made for sharing but this version is a feast for one. A plate piled high with the most delicious flavours – we start with a garlicky yoghurt which cools and warms all at once. Then it's onto a layer of lamb mince and soft aubergine fried in olive oil and spiced with cumin, coriander and cinnamon. Next, spoonfuls of the most luxurious toasted pine nut butter, finished with pops of sweet pomegranate seeds and all scooped up with toasted pitta bread. You'll be glad you're not sharing this one.

1 tbsp extra virgin olive oil
½ large aubergine (approx. 125g), sliced into 1cm batons
5 tbsp natural yoghurt
1 garlic clove, grated
125g lamb mince
1 tsp paprika
1 tsp ground cumin
½ tsp ground coriander
½ tsp ground cinnamon
5g fresh coriander, finely chopped
knob of butter
1½ tbsp pine nuts
3 tbsp pomegranate seeds
salt and black pepper

To serve:
pitta bread

Heat the olive oil in a pan over a medium-high heat, add the aubergine, season with salt and fry for 8–10 minutes until golden and mostly soft.

While that's frying, spoon the yoghurt onto your serving plate and add the garlic. Mix together and spread over the bottom of the plate.

Once the aubergine batons are golden, add in the lamb mince and fry for 4–5 minutes until brown and starting to crisp slightly. Add the spices and season with salt and pepper, then fry for 2–3 minutes. Toast the pitta bread while this is cooking. Add in the fresh coriander and mix everything together, then spoon the lamb and aubergine mixture over the yoghurt.

Place the pan back on the heat and add a knob of butter and the pine nuts. Let the nuts toast in the butter for 3–4 minutes until golden, then spoon them over the lamb/aubergine layer.

Sprinkle over the pomegranate seeds, then cut the pitta into triangles to serve alongside.

USE YOUR LEFTOVER:
lamb mince:
page 52 (in place
of beef mince)

For those days when all you need is something sweet. These recipes are for those pick-me-up moments when only an apple crumble, or a sticky toffee pudding will do. No need to wait until after dinner, enjoy these recipes at any time and indulge in the sweet joy of your favourite pudding. Fancy a cinnamon bun or a strawberry cheesecake for breakfast? I couldn't think of a better way to start the day.

SWEET

PEACH + CINNAMON COBBLER

Prep Time: 10 minutes
Cook Time: 25 minutes

I feel somewhat unqualified to speak on cobblers as they're not particularly common in the UK and as far as I understand it there are many different species of cobbler in the US, ranging from craggily, scone-like toppings to cake-like batters with crunchy edges. I've tried several cobblers and this version feels like a good hybrid of my favourite elements – crisp, sugar-coated edges and soft, jammy pockets where peach meets sponge, perfect for collecting pools of melting ice cream.

40g butter

40g plain flour

30g soft dark brown sugar

½ tsp ground cinnamon

¼ tsp vanilla extract

2 tbsp milk

½ tin peach slices, drained
  or 1 large fresh peach, sliced

1 tsp demerara sugar

To serve:
ice cream

Preheat the oven to 195°C (175°C fan).

Add the butter to an ovenproof frying pan or small baking dish and place in the oven while it's preheating just to melt the butter.

Once melted, add in the flour, dark brown sugar, cinnamon, vanilla and milk and stir everything together until well combined. Place the peach slices on top of the batter and press down slightly. Sprinkle over the demerara sugar, then bake in the oven for 25 minutes. Top with ice cream to serve.

USE YOUR LEFTOVER:

peach:
page 184

SELF-SAUCING STICKY TOFFEE PUDDING

Prep Time: 30 minutes
Cook Time: 35 minutes

All hail the sticky toffee pudding and its deep, rich, date-filled sponge and luscious, buttery caramel sauce. There's a reason it seems to be everyone's favourite pud. Despite its saccharine description, this manages not to be sickly thanks to the molasses flavour of dark brown sugar and a suggestion of spice from the black treacle. A scattering of salt at the end also helps balance the flavours. As with many recipes in this book, the easiest way to make this is to place your pan on the scales and weigh everything directly into it.

For the batter:

25g Medjool dates, pitted and
    chopped into small pieces
25g boiling water
¼ tsp vanilla extract
20g soft dark brown sugar
10g black treacle
15g butter, softened
25g self-raising flour
pinch of bicarbonate of soda
pinch of salt

For the sauce:

15g butter
15g soft dark brown sugar
50g boiling water

To serve:

flaky sea salt

Preheat the oven to 180°C (160°C fan).

Place the dates in a small pie dish or ovenproof frying pan. Cover with the 25g of boiling water and leave to sit for 20 minutes to soften the dates slightly.

Once soft, add in the rest of the ingredients for the batter and mix everything together thoroughly. Flatten out the batter slightly, then put small dollops of the butter and sugar for the sauce on top of the batter – don't mix them in. Gently pour over the 50g of boiling water so that it sits on top of the batter.

Bake for 35 minutes, then leave to cool for 10 minutes to allow the sauce to settle before eating. Sprinkle with flaky salt and serve.

USE YOUR LEFTOVER ... dates: page 156

LEMON BREAD + BUTTER PUDDING

If you ask me, bread and butter pudding is a 'proper pud'. Perhaps it's the northerner in me but I prefer my puddings warm, custardy and stodgy – in all the best ways. Though apple crumble will always be my number one dessert, bread and butter pudding is a strong contender for second place, though I really disagree with the traditional addition of dried fruit. No hate to raisins (ok, some hate to raisins...) but they're not welcome here. If you don't like lemon, you could happily use a chocolate hazelnut spread, marmalade or jam in place of the lemon curd.

Prep Time: 10 minutes
Cook Time: 30 minutes

Preheat the oven to 180°C (160°C fan).

Place a small ovenproof dish onto your scales, then weigh in all the ingredients apart from the bread and demerara sugar. Mix together until you have a smooth custard.

Add the cubes of bread to your custard mixture. Squish and mix everything together so the bread is fully covered in the custard and absorbs most of it. If using the demerara sugar, sprinkle a little over the top, then bake for 25–30 minutes until golden and slightly firm to the touch.

Serve with cream, ice cream or custard.

1 egg yolk
40g double cream
30g whole milk
splash of vanilla extract
20g caster sugar
25g lemon curd
zest of ½ lemon
2 slices of bread, around 50–65g,
   cut into 2cm squares
a little demerara sugar (optional)

To serve:
cream, ice cream or custard

USE YOUR LEFTOVER ...

egg white:
page 21

BAKED PEACHES WITH CARAMEL SAUCE

Prep Time: 5 minutes
Cook Time: 30 minutes

A ripe peach is truly one of life's greatest gifts, immediately transporting me to a sun-soaked summer holiday, toes dipped in a swimming pool and a napkin held up to your chin to catch the sweet juices of the season's best pick. Sorry, where were we? Ah yes, baked peaches with caramel sauce and roasty, toasty almonds. Another magical sort of dessert, it starts off feeling like not much will happen, but by the end the peach juice, butter and cream have created a sticky, amber caramel to pour over everything. The cardamom is optional, but I do love and highly recommend it.

1 fresh ripe peach/nectarine,
    sliced in half, stone removed
4 tsp soft light brown sugar
sprinkle of ground
    cardamom (optional)
20g butter
10g flaked almonds (or
    chopped pecans)
2 tbsp double cream

Preheat the oven to 180°C (160°C fan).

Place the peach in a small ovenproof dish. Sprinkle 2 teaspoons of the brown sugar, and the cardamom, if using, over each of the peach halves. Add 10g of butter to each half, then sprinkle the nuts around the peach halves. Bake in the oven for 30 minutes.

When baked, place the peach halves in your serving bowl. Add the double cream to the sugar, butter and nuts that are left in the dish. Mix together with a spoon or spatula until you have a smooth caramel. It will come together after a couple of minutes and any lumps of sugar will dissolve as you continue mixing.

Spoon the caramel over the peach halves before serving.

USE YOUR LEFTOVER:
double cream:
page 198

CHOCOLATE CHIP COOKIE SKILLET

Prep Time: 10 minutes
Cook Time: 15 minutes

Eating a whole skillet-sized cookie by yourself feels somewhat wrong and potentially indecent. How could this whole dish possibly be for one person? Well I'm here to tell you that it is. And it's ok. And you shouldn't let anyone else tell you otherwise. Decency is overrated, this cookie is not. You can vary the cooking time to make this as gooey and dough-like as you want, keeping it in for longer if you prefer more of a crisp crunch to your cookie.

40g softened butter
30g soft light brown sugar
25g granulated sugar
1 egg yolk
½ tsp vanilla extract
60g plain flour
¼ tsp baking powder
pinch of salt
30g chocolate chunks

To serve:
ice cream

Preheat the oven to 180°C (160°C fan).

Grab a small baking dish or ovenproof frying pan and add in your softened butter and both types of sugar. Mix together until smooth, then add the egg yolk and vanilla extract and mix again. Add in the plain flour, baking powder and salt and mix together until you have a smooth dough. Finally, add in the chocolate chunks and combine until evenly distributed.

Bake in the oven for 12–15 minutes or until golden and slightly gooey in the middle.

Serve with your favourite ice cream.

USE YOUR LEFTOVER ...

egg white:
page 188

CHOCOLATE BROWNIE

Prep Time: 10 minutes
Cook Time: 10–25 minutes

I couldn't have a sweet chapter without a chocolate brownie now could I? I fully support you if you decide that a whole tray of brownies is more your style, but if you're looking for a single hit of chocolate, then this might be the recipe for you. One for the sweet-toothers among us, you can customise this brownie to suit your every need. Keep it molten in the middle for a chocolate fondant effect, or, if you prefer your brownies chewy, leave it a little longer in the oven.

40g butter
40g chocolate, broken into pieces
45g caster sugar
25g plain flour
10g cocoa powder
pinch of salt
1 egg white
flaky sea salt, for sprinkling

Preheat the oven to 180°C (160°C fan).

In a small ovenproof dish, add the butter and the chocolate pieces. Place in the oven for a couple of minutes, just until the butter and chocolate have softened. Take out the dish and mix the butter and chocolate together until smooth and all the chocolate has melted.

Add in the sugar and mix again. Add in the flour, cocoa powder and salt and mix until thick and smooth. Finally, add in the egg white and mix until smooth and glossy. Smooth out with your spatula/the back of your spoon, then bake in the oven. If you are using a wider dish (e.g. a small pie dish), where the brownie is flat and has a larger surface area, you will only need to bake it for around 10 minutes; if you are using a small, deeper dish (such as an individual-sized casserole dish), you will need to bake it for around 25 minutes.

Bake until the edges of the brownie are set but the middle has a nice soft jiggle to it. Once baked, sprinkle over some flaky salt and let it cool slightly before eating.

USE YOUR LEFTOVER...

egg yolk:
page 202

APPLE TARTE TATIN

Tarte Tatin has an air of sophistication about it that brings with it a reputation for being difficult or time-consuming to make. In reality, it's uncomplicated and undemanding, especially if you use ready-rolled pastry. You can keep the apples chunkier so they retain more structure and texture when baked, or slice them thinly and they'll melt down to an almost jammy consistency which mingles with the caramel. Either way, serve with a generous dollop of something cold and creamy.

Prep Time: 15 minutes
Cook Time: 30 minutes

Preheat the oven to 180°C (160°C fan).

Unroll your pastry sheet and cut it into a circle the size of the cast-iron frying pan or skillet you will use to cook this.

Add the sugar to your pan and heat over a medium heat. Don't stir it but let it melt, then gently swill it around the pan as it turns to liquid. It will start to caramelise and turn a golden colour, this will take 4–5 minutes.

Once the sugar is golden, turn off the heat and add in the butter (this won't be the final colour of the caramel as it will continue to cook in the oven). The butter will froth up slightly, so be careful as you stir it together. Add in the vanilla and a small pinch of salt and stir again to combine everything.

Once combined, place the apple slices on top of the caramel, arranging them in any way you like but trying to keep them in one single layer as much as possible. Lay the circle of pastry on top of the apples and tuck it around the edges of the pan slightly. Place in the oven and bake for 25 minutes or until the pastry is crisp and golden.

Once baked, take your serving plate and place it face down on top of the pan. Carefully but confidently flip the plate and pan over, turning out the tarte so the apples are now facing up. Serve with whipped cream, ice cream or crème fraîche.

75g ready-rolled puff pastry

35g caster sugar

30g butter

¼ tsp vanilla extract

small pinch of salt

140g baking apple (around 1 small apple), peeled, cored and cut into 1cm slices

To serve:

whipped cream, ice cream or crème fraîche

USE YOUR LEFTOVER

puff pastry:
page 40

BROWN SUGAR PLUM PIE

Prep Time: 15 minutes
Cook Time: 30 minutes

Hold an entire pie between two hands, then tell me you don't feel a sort of medieval power come upon you. A mug of mead completes the effect, though this is harder to come by. We may not have mead, or medieval power, but we do have plums! Joyous, juicy plums. Pile them high and surround them with buttery, golden pastry and a scatter of crunchy demerara. Because you're cutting circles from the pastry, you will need a full sheet; however, you can squish the remains together and use them in another recipe (see page 222 for ideas).

100g ready-rolled shortcrust pastry
2 plums, cut in half
    and stones removed
2 tsp soft light brown sugar
½ tsp plain flour
small knob of softened butter
1 egg yolk (optional)
1 tsp demerara sugar

Preheat the oven to 180°C (160°C fan). Line a small baking tray with baking paper.

Unroll the pastry and cut out two circles, each around 15cm in diameter. Place one circle on the lined baking tray.

Place the four plum halves (cut-side down) on this circle of pastry, piling them up and overlapping them slightly to create a mound of plums, and leaving a few centimetres of border around the edge. Sprinkle over the light brown sugar and the flour, then place a small knob of butter on top. Lay the other circle of pastry over the plums, then bring the two edges of the pastry together and crimp them by pinching together and rolling in towards the plums.

If you have a leftover egg yolk, then brush this over the top of the pastry; however, if you don't have a spare egg, then you could use a little extra softened butter or simply some water. Sprinkle over the demerara sugar, then cut a small hole in the top of the pastry to let the steam out.

Bake for 30 minutes or until golden.

USE YOUR LEFTOVER:
shortcrust pastry:
page 158

GINGER + LIME POACHED PEAR

Prep Time: 5 minutes
Cook Time: 45 minutes

Poached pears stick in my mind as a dinner party dessert. However, if you've bought this book, and you're considering making this recipe, you're probably not having a dinner party, but don't worry, they taste just as good on your own. Anyway, biblical miracles aside, I'm not sure one lonesome pear would go far in satisfying a table of guests, so you can enjoy this one all to yourself. The ginger can be fiery, so remove the pieces before eating if you don't want as much heat.

300ml water
40g soft brown sugar
10g fresh ginger, peeled
 and cut into strips
1 lime
½ tsp vanilla paste
1 pear, peeled, sliced in half
 lengthways and cored

To serve:
crème fraîche or ice cream

In a small saucepan, add the water, sugar, ginger, the juice of the lime and the vanilla paste. Bring to the boil, then simmer until the sugar has dissolved.

Add the pear halves to the syrup, then simmer for 40 minutes until the pear halves are tender but not completely soft.

Place the pear halves in your serving bowl and spoon over the syrupy glaze. Finish with a grating of the lime zest and serve with a spoonful of crème fraîche or ice cream.

USE YOUR LEFTOVER...

ginger:
page 64

MARYLAND COOKIE CAKE

I have my grandma and my brother to thank for this recipe. I remember them making a larger version of this cake when I was younger and I was so jealous that my brother got to make it and not me! How dare he? Well look at me now, claiming this recipe as my own. How's that for sibling rivalry? Their version involved sandwiching the soaked cookies together with cream in a horizontal log, almost as if you were bricklaying, before covering the entire log in more cream and finishing it with grated chocolate. I've restructured this slightly for ease and the result is almost, dare I say, reminiscent of the flavours of tiramisu.

Prep Time: 10 minutes
Cook Time: 0 minutes

Make the coffee in a medium heatproof bowl. Let it cool slightly, then take a cookie and dip it into the coffee, soaking it for a couple of seconds on each side. Place the cookie in a small glass and repeat with the rest of the cookies. Spoon over a little more coffee, then discard any excess coffee left in the bowl.

Add the cream to the bowl along with the vanilla. Whisk until you have soft peaks, then spoon the cream over the cookies.

Scatter over the grated chocolate, then either eat the cake straight away or keep it in the fridge to chill slightly.

50ml brewed coffee/1 shot
  of espresso
5 small chocolate chip cookies
70g double cream
¼ tsp vanilla paste

To serve:
1 square of dark chocolate, grated

USE YOUR LEFTOVER...
double cream:
page 144

STRAWBERRY CHEESECAKE

Prep Time: 15 minutes
Chill Time: 60 minutes

Technically this is an upside-down strawberry cheesecake, but I'm sure you'll forgive technicalities when you taste this pot. I prefer my cheesecakes light and airy, with fresh and fruity flavours. I've opted for shortbread, because the high proportion of butter means no additional fat is needed for the biscuit base/topping. I recommend chilling the cheesecake for at least an hour but, if you can't wait, it will still be delicious eaten straight away. It also comes together in mere moments, but you'd never know from the result.

30g double cream
45g full-fat cream cheese
30g icing sugar
¼ tsp vanilla paste
7 strawberries
2 shortbread fingers (45g)

Add the cream to a small glass and whisk up using a small whisk or a fork until you have fairly stiff peaks.

Add the cream cheese, icing sugar and vanilla and whisk together until smooth.

Take 6 of the strawberries and finely chop them, running your knife back and forth through the strawberries until you have a chunky purée. Add this to the cream mixture and stir through until incorporated.

Take your shortbread fingers and chop them up in the same way as the strawberries, running your knife back and forth through them until you have fine crumbs. Sprinkle these on top of the cheesecake mixture and gently press them down to compact them slightly.

Chill in the fridge for at least an hour, then slice the final strawberry and set on top of the cheesecake before serving.

USE YOUR LEFTOVER...
cream cheese:
page 116

CARDAMOM + COCONUT RICE PUDDING WITH MANGO

Prep Time: 5 minutes
Cook Time: 35 minutes

Sweet-toothers, assemble (again). This is my one-pot, one-portion coconut and cardamom rice pudding with mango, to be enjoyed warm or cold. A recurring spice in many of my recipes, I adore the flavour of cardamom and here it provides a foundation of subtle spice, bringing warmth and sweetness to the dessert. Using coconut milk instead of dairy milk makes the pudding even creamier, and the fresh mango on top cuts through the rich rice perfectly. Thank goodness this is only one portion, as you won't want to share this.

50g risotto rice
200ml coconut milk
200ml water
25g caster sugar
3 cardamom pods, left whole
¼ tsp vanilla extract

To serve:
½ small ripe mango, finely sliced
maple syrup (optional)

Add all the ingredients for the rice pudding to a saucepan and bring to a gentle boil over a medium heat.

Turn the heat down and simmer for 25–30 minutes or until the rice has fully cooked, stirring frequently. If it gets too thick, add a little extra water.

When the rice pudding is done, serve it up with the mango slices placed on top and a drizzle of maple syrup, if you like.

USE YOUR LEFTOVER...
coconut milk:
page 70

CHOCOLATE POT

Prep Time: 5 minutes
Chill Time: 60 minutes

Look up decadence in the dictionary and you'll see a picture of this pot. I can't fully describe the silky, smooth, richness of this dessert, so you're just going to have to make it for yourself and see. Though any dark chocolate will do, I lean towards a lower percentage of cocoa, around 50%, as I enjoy the subtle sweetness that balances the bitter notes. I can't help but top this with squirty cream, a child-like joy that some may turn their nose up at, but there's no place for snobbery in this book. Lean into the youthful joy that this treat brings.

50g double cream
50g dark chocolate (50–70% cocoa),
   broken into pieces
1 egg yolk
pinch of salt

To serve:
squirty cream, crème fraîche or
   whipped cream
finely chopped or grated chocolate

Add the double cream to a saucepan and heat over a low heat until it barely begins to simmer, then take it off the heat.

Add the chocolate pieces to the cream and stir together, allowing the heat of the cream to melt the chocolate. Keep stirring until it's fully melted and incorporated into the cream.

Add the egg yolk and a pinch of salt to the chocolate mixture and stir until smooth. Pour into a small ramekin or glass and chill in the fridge for 1 hour.

Serve topped with your cream of choice and a little finely chopped or grated chocolate.

USE YOUR LEFTOVER

double cream:
page 24

BANOFFEE PIE MILKSHAKE

My auntie lives near Bath and when I was growing up, there was a milkshake shop where you could choose flavours and toppings from an entire wall of sweet treats. I'm talking hundreds of choices, or at least that's what it felt like as a child staring up at the almost celestial display. My milkshake flavour of choice was Daim bar because of the caramelly crunch throughout and this banoffee pie milkshake has a similar vibe, with chunks of chocolate digestive breaking up the banana toffee milk. There's absolutely no cooking, prep work or real skill involved here, I almost feel guilty calling it a recipe, but it is perfect for when you need a sweet hit in the next 5 minutes.

Prep Time: 5 minutes
Cook Time: 0 minutes

Add the banana, maple syrup/caramel sauce, salt, ice cream and milk to a blender and blend until smooth.

Once smooth, break in the chocolate digestives, leaving a little aside for the top. Blitz again just for a few seconds until the digestives are mostly broken up but still a little chunky.

Pour the milkshake into a glass and top with squirty cream, then crumble over the leftover biscuit and serve.

1 banana, peeled
1 tbsp maple syrup/caramel sauce
pinch of salt
2 scoops of vanilla or banana ice cream
5 tbsp milk
2 chocolate digestives
squirty cream

USE YOUR LEFTOVER...

ice cream: page 216

MAPLE NUT GRANOLA

Prep Time: 5 minutes
Cook Time: 10 minutes

I wanted to include a recipe in this chapter that provided sweetness without necessarily being a dessert. I'm not saying you couldn't eat crumble or sticky toffee pudding for breakfast (hopefully at this point in the book you know that I would fully endorse this), but just in case you don't fancy that, my maple nut granola provides an alternative. This doesn't crisp up until it cools down, so don't be alarmed if it's still soft in the pan. You'll know it's done from the toasted, maple smell and when the colour changes from pale to dark golden.

30g porridge oats
2 tbsp maple syrup
10g butter
pinch of salt
30g pecans or other nuts,
  roughly chopped

Add everything to a frying pan and cook over a low heat for 8–10 minutes, stirring occasionally, until the oats and the nuts are golden and smell toasted.

Pour into a bowl to cool down and crisp up.

USE YOUR LEFTOVER
pecans:
page 214

CHOCOLATE + HAZELNUT FILO ROLLS

Roll up, roll up all you Nutella lovers. I couldn't resist creating something heavenly for those of us with a deep love for that well-known chocolate and hazelnut combination, but with a one-pot one-portion twist. These chocolate hazelnut filo rolls will satisfy just about any craving, they're quick and easy to make and perfect for any occasion. Dips are optional but wholly encouraged. Double-dunk into a jar of Nutella? I will if you will...

Prep Time: 10 minutes
Cook Time: 5 minutes

Cut the sheet of filo into quarters. Spoon 1 teaspoon of chocolate and hazelnut spread along the long length of one filo quarter. Fold the two sides of the filo over to seal the edges, then roll up into a straw. Brush the edge of the filo with a little water to seal. Repeat with all four quarters until you have four straws.

Place a couple of pieces of kitchen roll on your chopping board.

Heat 1–2cm of oil in a small pan over a medium-high heat. Once hot, add the straws, frying for a minute or two on each side until golden. Take the straws out of the oil and let them cool on the kitchen roll to remove any excess oil.

Place on your serving plate and sprinkle over a little caster sugar before serving with Nutella or caramel sauce.

1 sheet of filo pastry
4 tsp chocolate and hazelnut spread (I use Nutella)
vegetable oil
caster sugar, for sprinkling

To serve:
extra Nutella or caramel sauce

USE YOUR LEFTOVER...

filo pastry:
page 214

APPLE CRUMBLE

Prep Time: 10 minutes
Cook Time: 30 minutes

Apple crumble is my favourite pudding of all time. If I could only eat one dessert for the rest of my life, it would be this one, preferably with gallons of warm, ambrosial custard. I have strong opinions on most things but particularly on what makes the perfect crumble. I think there should be a 50:50 ratio of fruit to crumble topping and, when it comes to said topping, I want the top to be crunchy whilst the bit that touches the fruit needs to be stodgy. You can add cinnamon, or a sprinkle of oats on top, but I am a purist when it comes to this pud and really don't want anything other than apples, and buttery crumble. I hope you enjoy this as much as I do.

1 small apple (approx. 100g), peeled, cored and cut into 1cm dice
1 tbsp water
20g caster sugar
30g butter
40g plain flour

To serve:
ice cream, cream or custard

Preheat the oven to 195°C (175°C fan).

Add the apple to a small baking dish with the water.

In a bowl, combine the caster sugar, butter and flour. Rub the butter into the flour and sugar until you have a crumbly texture. Place the crumble on top of the apple and press down slightly.

Bake for 30 minutes until golden.

Serve with ice cream, cream or custard.

USE YOUR LEFTOVER...
apples:
page 191

CINNAMON BUN

Prep Time: 15 minutes
Cook Time: 30 minutes

This is the easiest cinnamon bun recipe you may ever find, relying on no dough, no yeast, no kneading and no proving time. I use ready-made puff pastry here to make the bun and, whilst usually you want to keep puff pastry as flaky and delicate as possible, for this recipe you're actually looking for the centre of this pastry to melt together to create a consistency more akin to a yeasted dough. It stays crisp on top too, which I love.

80–85g ready-rolled puff pastry
10g softened butter, plus extra
for greasing
3 tsp soft light brown sugar
½ tsp ground cinnamon

Preheat the oven to 180°C (160°C fan).

Unroll the puff pastry and cut off a long strip that is 5cm in width. Spread the butter on top of the pastry, then sprinkle the sugar and cinnamon over the top.

Fold the pastry over so it halves in length, then press together to seal slightly. Cut into three strips. At one end, press the three strips together, then plait the strips, taking one outside strip and bringing it into the middle, then bring the other outside strip into the middle, repeating until the end.

Lightly butter one hole of a muffin tin, or a small ovenproof ramekin, then roll the plait up and place it in the tin/ramekin with the loose end at the bottom of the tin/ramekin. Bake for 25–30 minutes until golden.

USE YOUR LEFTOVER …
puff pastry:
page 40

HONEY NUT FILO PARCELS

Prep Time: 15 minutes
Cook Time: 15 minutes

Baklava is a well-known Middle Eastern dessert consisting of syrup-soaked layers of filo pastry and chopped, spiced nuts. It's heavenly, and it's where the inspiration for this recipe comes from, though it's not entirely the same as my version. These parcels are filled with chopped pistachios and pecans, though in theory you could use other nuts too, encased in buttery filo, then covered in honey while still warm, so it oozes through the layers to give a sticky, sweet finish.

15g pistachios, finely chopped
15g pecans, finely chopped
1 sheet of filo pastry
4 tsp butter, plus extra for greasing
2 tsp honey

Preheat the oven to 195°C (175°C fan).

Combine the pistachios and the pecans in a bowl. Cut the filo sheet in half, then cut each half into quarters.

Grease two holes of a muffin tin with a little butter, then layer up four pieces of filo into each hole, overlapping each piece. Spoon half of the nuts into each hole, then add 1 teaspoon of butter on top of each set of nuts. Fold the edges of the filo over the nuts and press into the butter to seal. Spoon another teaspoon of butter on top of the filo, then cut a large cross in each parcel, cutting through to the nuts to allow the butter to soak in.

Bake in the oven for 10–15 minutes until golden and crisp.

Once cooked, and while still warm, spoon 1 teaspoon of honey over each parcel and let that soak into the pastry and nuts while they cool down.

USE YOUR LEFTOVER...

filo pastry:
page 209

SELF-SAUCING CHOCOLATE MUG CAKE

Prep Time: 5 minutes
Cook Time: 5 minutes

Another classic in the one-pot, one-portion repertoire, I spent hours and hours developing this, despite it being such a simplistic concept. It's that simplicity that necessitates perfection and I think I've achieved that. Boiling water is the magic ingredient here. It enriches the sponge itself, providing moisture and bringing out the flavour of the cocoa, as well as being the basis for the sauce. The sauce itself forms as the cake cooks, mingling with the sugar and the cocoa. As this is a microwave cake, much of the cooking technique relies on the equipment you're using, and the cake will need different times in different microwaves. You might need to make this a few times before perfecting it, but if you ask me, that may not be such a bad thing. The ice cream is mandatory, ok?

For the sponge:

25g butter

25g granulated sugar

30g self-raising flour

10g cocoa powder

pinch of salt

20g boiling water

For the sauce:

10g granulated sugar

5g cocoa powder

25g boiling water

To serve:

vanilla ice cream

Place a microwave-safe mug on your scales. Measure the butter into the mug, then melt this in the microwave for 30 seconds or so.

Weigh in the sugar, flour and cocoa powder and add the salt. Mix together, then add the boiling water and mix again until you have a smooth batter.

Next, make the sauce. Smooth out the batter until flat, then sprinkle the sugar and cocoa powder in an even layer over the cake mix. Gently pour over the boiling water, trying to cover the sugar and cocoa without mixing the water into the cake batter. You can swirl the mug to distribute the water more evenly.

Microwave on low for 1–5 minutes, depending on the power of your microwave. You want the sponge to have risen slightly and be sort of firm to the touch, but fudgy and saucy around the edges.

Serve with a big scoop of vanilla ice cream.

USE YOUR LEFTOVER...
ice cream:
page 205

Ingredient Index

apple: apple crumble 210
apple tarte tatin 191
roast pork belly with apple
+ shallot gravy 168
satay slaw with curried
chicken skewers 84

aubergine: aubergine parmy 18
spiced lamb + aubergine
with pitta 174

avocado: chicken, mango
+ avocado tacos with
lime crema 73
chipotle pulled chicken
with avocado + tomato salsa
+ tortilla chips 89
hash brown breakfast
skillet 129
kale, salmon + sweet potato
salad with a creamy garlic
dressing 114
peanut noodle salad 90
tuna tostadas with avocado,
jalapeños + pickled ginger 141

bacon: bacon + potato gratin 163
risotto carbonara 38
roast chicken with sage, onion
+ chestnut stuffing 166

beans *see* butter beans;
cannellini beans;
kidney beans

beef mince: chilli con carne
con rice 42
hash brown cottage pie 52
lasagne 26
smash burger flatbread 111

bread: courgette carpaccio
with crispy capers + butter
beans 61
creamy scrambled eggs
with cottage cheese 124
fish finger sandwich with
crispy capers 122
French onion soup 150
halloumi or cod Provençal 81
lemon bread + butter
pudding 183
prawn + chorizo pil pil 132
prawn toastie 46
steak + crisp sandwich
with chimichurri 138
see also flatbread

broccoli: chicken + broccoli
alfredo 22
creamy green linguine 106
curried gnocchi, corn
+ tomato bake 67
ginger chicken rice bowl 64
green curry coconut rice 92
gyoza stir fry 108

butter beans: brothy pasta
with beans + greens 100
courgette carpaccio with crispy
capers + butter beans 61

butternut squash: caramelised
onion, squash + goat's cheese
tarte tatin 40
creamy baked gnocchi with
squash + sausage 32
pumpkin curry 29
toad in the hole 37

cabbage: roast pork belly with
apple + shallot gravy 168
satay slaw with curried chicken
skewers 84
vegetable pancake with
a chilli crisp egg 98

cannellini beans: brothy pasta
with beans + greens 100

capers: courgette carpaccio
with crispy capers + butter
beans 61
fish finger sandwich with
crispy capers 122
halloumi or cod Provençal 81

carrot: hash brown cottage
pie 52
peanut noodle salad 90
pickled vegetable salad with
soy-glazed meatballs 78
roast chicken with sage, onion
+ chestnut stuffing 166
roast pork belly with apple
+ shallot gravy 168
tortellini + sausage soup 120
vegetable pancake with
a chilli crisp egg 98

cashews: curried gnocchi, corn
+ tomato bake 67
green curry coconut rice 92
herby chicken + rice salad 68

Cheddar: croque madame
pastry 116
fish pie 30
hash brown breakfast
skillet 129
loaded jacket potato 112

mac + cheese with
crispy onions 54

chicken breast: chicken
+ broccoli alfredo 22
chicken Caesar salad with
chicken-fat panko crumbs 62
chicken, mango + avocado
tacos with lime crema 73
chicken parmy 18
chicken + sweetcorn soup 104
chipotle pulled chicken with
avocado + tomato salsa
+ tortilla chips 89
ginger chicken rice bowl 64
green curry coconut rice 92
herby chicken + rice salad 68
roast chicken with sage, onion
+ chestnut stuffing 166
satay slaw with curried chicken
skewers 84
tarragon chicken with leeks,
peas + potatoes 48
Tuscan chicken + potato 164
chicken thigh: chicken Caesar
salad with chicken-fat panko
crumbs 62
chicken or paneer biryani 148
chicken + prawn paella 172
chicken, sweetcorn + leek
pot pie 45
jerk chicken with coconut
rice + pineapple 82
chickpeas: brothy pasta with
beans + greens 100
chickpea, turmeric + coconut
curry 130
chilli: chilaquiles with egg
+ feta 76
chilli con carne con rice 42
crispy chilli beef noodles 21
peanut noodle salad 90
pickled vegetable salad with
soy-glazed meatballs 78
pork + ginger lettuce wraps 94
prawn + chorizo pil pil 132
satay slaw with curried chicken
skewers 84

sausage, fennel + chilli pasta 16
spiced lamb steak with
coriander + date chutney 156
steak + crisp sandwich with
chimichurri 138
vegetable pancake with a chilli
crisp egg 98
chocolate: chocolate brownie 188
chocolate chip cookie
skillet 186
chocolate pot 202
Maryland cookie cake 197
self-saucing chocolate
mug cake 216
chorizo: chorizo, potato
+ feta frittata 102
loaded jacket potato 112
prawn + chorizo pil pil 132
coconut milk: cardamom
+ coconut rice pudding
with mango 200
chickpea, turmeric
+ coconut curry 130
green curry coconut rice 92
jerk chicken with coconut
rice + pineapple 82
peanut curry with tofu
+ potatoes 34
salmon, coconut +
lemongrass noodles 70
satay slaw with curried
chicken skewers 84
coconut yoghurt: curried
gnocchi, corn + tomato
bake 67
herby chicken + rice
salad 68
cod: fish pie 30
halloumi or cod Provençal 81
corn on the cob: Cajun shrimp
boil 160
curried gnocchi, corn
+ tomato bake 67
see also sweetcorn
courgette: courgette carpaccio
with crispy capers + butter
beans 61

vegetable pancake with a chilli
crisp egg 98
cream cheese: chicken, sweetcorn
+ leek pot pie 45
creamy baked gnocchi with
squash + sausage 32
croque madame pastry 116
strawberry cheesecake 198
crème fraîche: apple tarte
tatin 191
chocolate pot 202
fish pie 30
ginger + lime poached pear 194
crispy onions: chicken
or paneer biryani 148
mac + cheese with
crispy onions 54
cucumber: jerk chicken with
coconut rice + pineapple 82
pickled vegetable salad with
soy-glazed meatballs 78

dates: self-saucing sticky toffee
pudding 180
spiced lamb steak with
coriander + date chutney 156
double cream: bacon
+ potato gratin 163
baked peaches with
caramel sauce 184
chicken + broccoli alfredo 22
chocolate pot 202
lemon bread + butter
pudding 183
lobster spaghetti with
lemon + tomatoes 144
Maryland cookie cake 197
matar paneer 24
strawberry cheesecake 198
tarragon chicken with
leeks, peas + potatoes 48
Tuscan chicken + potato 164

egg white: chocolate brownie 188
crispy chilli beef noodles 21
egg yolk: brown sugar plum
pie 192

chicken, sweetcorn
    + leek pot pie 45
chocolate chip cookie
    skillet 186
chocolate pot 202
lemon bread + butter
    pudding 183
risotto carbonara 38
eggs, whole: chicken
    + sweetcorn soup 104
chilaquiles with egg
    + feta 76
chorizo, potato + feta
    frittata 102
creamy green linguine 106
creamy scrambled eggs
    with cottage cheese 124
croque madame pastry 116
hash brown breakfast
    skillet 129
risotto carbonara 38
toad in the hole 37
vegetable pancake with
    a chilli crisp egg 98

feta cheese: chilaquiles
    with egg + feta 76
chorizo, potato + feta
    frittata 102
filo pastry: chocolate +
    hazelnut filo rolls 209
honey nut filo parcels 214
flatbread: chickpea, turmeric
    + coconut curry 130
pork + pineapple flatbread 86
smash burger flatbread 111

gnocchi: creamy baked gnocchi
    with squash + sausage 32
curried gnocchi, corn + tomato
    bake 67
gnocchi con tomate 119
tortellini + sausage soup 120
gochujang: cheesy gochujang
    noodles 126
pork + pineapple
    flatbread 86

ham: chicken parmy 18
croque madame pastry 116
hash browns: hash brown
    breakfast skillet 129
hash brown cottage pie 52

kale: kale, salmon + sweet potato
    salad with a creamy garlic
    dressing 114
tortellini + sausage soup 120
kidney beans: chilli con carne
    con rice 42
jerk chicken with coconut rice
    + pineapple 82

lamb: spiced lamb + aubergine
    with pitta 174
spiced lamb steak with
    coriander + date chutney 156
leeks: chicken, sweetcorn
    + leek pot pie 45
marmalade sausage
    traybake 134
tarragon chicken with leeks,
    peas + potatoes 48
lemon: cajun shrimp boil 160
chicken + prawn paella 172
chicken Caesar salad
    with chicken-fat panko
    crumbs 62
courgette carpaccio with crispy
    capers + butter beans 61
creamy green linguine 106
curried gnocchi, corn + tomato
    bake 67
fish finger sandwich with
    crispy capers 122
herby chicken + rice salad 68
kale, salmon + sweet potato
    salad with a creamy garlic
    dressing 114
lemon bread + butter
    pudding 183
lobster spaghetti with lemon
    + tomatoes 144
peach + burrata orzo salad 59
prawn + chorizo pil pil 132

lettuce: chicken Caesar salad with
    chicken-fat panko crumbs 62
fish finger sandwich with
    crispy capers 122
pork + ginger lettuce wraps 94
smash burger flatbread 111
lime: chicken, mango + avocado
    tacos with lime crema 73
chilli con carne con rice 42
chipotle pulled chicken
    with avocado + tomato salsa
    + tortilla chips 89
ginger + lime poached pear 194
gyoza stir fry 108
hash brown breakfast
    skillet 129
peanut curry with tofu
    + potatoes 34
peanut noodle salad 90
pork + ginger lettuce wraps 94
satay slaw with curried chicken
    skewers 84
tuna tostadas with avocado,
    jalapeños + pickled ginger 141

mango: cardamom + coconut rice
    pudding with mango 200
chicken, mango + avocado
    tacos with lime crema 73
mascarpone: lasagne 26
truffled mushroom
    pappardelle 147
meatballs: meatball +
    mozzarella orzo 51
pickled vegetable salad with
    soy-glazed meatballs 78
mozzarella: cheesy gochujang
    noodles 126
chicken, mango + avocado
    tacos with lime crema 73
chicken parmy 18
chilaquiles with egg + feta 76
hash brown breakfast
    skillet 129
lasagne 26
mac + cheese with
    crispy onions 54

meatball + mozzarella orzo 51

mortadella + mozzarella
    focaccia 142

salami + hot honey frying
    pan pizza 152

mushrooms: beef Wellington
    with roasted potatoes
    + onions 158

truffled mushroom
    pappardelle 147

noodles: cheesy gochujang
    noodles 126

crispy chilli beef noodles 21

peanut noodle salad 90

salmon, coconut + lemongrass
    noodles 70

onions: beef Wellington
    with roasted potatoes
    + onions 158

caramelised onion, squash +
    goat's cheese tarte tatin 40

French onion soup 150

roast chicken with sage, onion
    + chestnut stuffing 166

see also crispy onions

paneer: chicken or paneer
    biryani 148

matar paneer 24

Parmesan: brothy pasta
    with beans + greens 100

chicken + broccoli alfredo 22

chicken Caesar salad with
    chicken-fat panko crumbs 62

chicken parmy 18

fresh pici pasta with pesto 155

lobster spaghetti with lemon
    + tomatoes 144

risotto carbonara 38

truffled mushroom
    pappardelle 147

parsnips: roast chicken with sage,
    onion + chestnut stuffing 166

roast pork belly with apple
    + shallot gravy 168

passata: matar paneer 24

salami + hot honey frying pan
    pizza 152

pasta: brothy pasta with
    beans + greens 100

chicken + broccoli alfredo 22

creamy green linguine 106

fresh pici pasta with pesto 155

lasagne 26

lobster spaghetti with lemon
    + tomatoes 144

mac + cheese with crispy
    onions 54

meatball + mozzarella orzo 51

peach + burrata orzo salad 59

roasted red pepper, tomato
    + preserved lemon orzo 74

sausage, fennel + chilli
    pasta 16

tortellini + sausage soup 120

truffled mushroom
    pappardelle 147

pastry see filo pastry; puff
    pastry; shortcrust pastry

peaches: baked peaches with
    caramel sauce 184

peach + burrata orzo salad 59

peach + cinnamon cobbler 178

peanut butter: peanut curry with
    tofu + potatoes 34

satay slaw with curried chicken
    skewers 84

peanuts: gyoza stir fry 108

peanut curry with tofu
    + potatoes 34

peanut noodle salad 90

satay slaw with curried
    chicken skewers 84

peas: chorizo, potato
    + feta frittata 102

fish pie 30

hash brown cottage pie 52

matar paneer 24

roast chicken with sage, onion
    + chestnut stuffing 166

tarragon chicken with leeks,
    peas + potatoes 48

pecans: baked peaches with
    caramel sauce 184

caramelised onion, squash
    + goat's cheese tarte tatin 40

honey nut filo parcels 214

maple nut granola 206

pecorino: creamy green
    linguine 106

sausage, fennel + chilli pasta 16

peppers see red peppers

pineapple: jerk chicken with
    coconut rice + pineapple 82

pork + pineapple flatbread 86

pork: pork + pineapple
    flatbread 86

roast pork belly with apple
    + shallot gravy 168

pork mince: pickled vegetable
    salad with soy-glazed
    meatballs 78

pork + ginger lettuce wraps 94

potatoes: bacon + potato
    gratin 163

beef Wellington with roasted
    potatoes + onions 158

Cajun shrimp boil 160

chorizo, potato + feta
    frittata 102

fish pie 30

loaded jacket potato 112

marmalade sausage
    traybake 134

peanut curry with tofu
    + potatoes 34

roast chicken with sage, onion
    + chestnut stuffing 166

roast pork belly with apple
    + shallot gravy 168

spiced lamb steak with
    coriander + date chutney 156

tarragon chicken with leeks,
    peas + potatoes 48

toad in the hole 37

Tuscan chicken + potato 164

prawns: Cajun shrimp boil 160

chicken + prawn paella 172

prawn + chorizo pil pil 132

prawn toastie 46
puff pastry: apple tarte tatin 191
  caramelised onion, squash +
    goat's cheese tarte tatin 40
  cinnamon bun 212
  croque madame pastry 116

red peppers: chicken
    + prawn paella 172
  crispy chilli beef noodles 21
  gyoza stir fry 108
  halloumi or cod Provençal 81
  marmalade sausage
    traybake 134
  peanut noodle salad 90
  roasted red pepper, tomato
    + preserved lemon orzo 74
rice: cardamom + coconut rice
    pudding with mango 200
  chicken or paneer biryani 148
  chicken + prawn paella 172
  chilli con carne con rice 42
  ginger chicken rice bowl 64
  green curry coconut rice 92
  herby chicken + rice salad 68
  jerk chicken with coconut rice
    + pineapple 82
  pork + ginger lettuce wraps 94
  risotto carbonara 38

salmon: fish pie 30
  kale, salmon + sweet potato
    salad with a creamy garlic
    dressing 114
  salmon, coconut + lemongrass
    noodles 70
sausages: creamy baked gnocchi
    with squash + sausage 32
  marmalade sausage
    traybake 134
  pork + kimchi steamed
    buns 171
  roast chicken with sage, onion
    + chestnut stuffing 166
  sausage, fennel + chilli pasta 16
  toad in the hole 37
  tortellini + sausage soup 120

shallots: roast chicken with sage,
    onion + chestnut stuffing 166
  roast pork belly with apple
    + shallot gravy 168
shortcrust pastry: beef
    Wellington with roasted
    potatoes + onions 158
  brown sugar plum pie 192
  chicken, sweetcorn + leek
    pot pie 45
sour cream: chicken, mango
    + avocado tacos with lime
    crema 73
  chilaquiles with egg + feta 76
  chilli con carne con rice 42
  loaded jacket potato 112
  tuna tostadas with avocado,
    jalapeños + pickled
    ginger 141
spinach: brothy pasta with
    beans + greens 100
  creamy green linguine 106
  tortellini + sausage soup 120
  Tuscan chicken + potato 164
steak: beef Wellington
    with roasted potatoes
    + onions 158
  crispy chilli beef noodles 21
  steak + crisp sandwich
    with chimichurri 138
sweet potato: kale, salmon
    + sweet potato salad with
    a creamy garlic dressing 114
sweetcorn: chicken + sweetcorn
    soup 104
  chicken, sweetcorn + leek pot
    pie 45
  see also corn on the cob

tofu: green curry coconut rice 92
  peanut curry with tofu
    + potatoes 34
tomatoes, fresh: chicken
    + prawn paella 172
  chipotle pulled chicken
    with avocado + tomato salsa
    + tortilla chips 89

creamy baked gnocchi with
    squash + sausage 32
  curried gnocchi, corn + tomato
    bake 67
  gnocchi con tomate 119
  halloumi or cod Provençal 81
  lobster spaghetti with lemon
    + tomatoes 144
  marmalade sausage
    traybake 134
  peach + burrata orzo salad 59
  roasted red pepper, tomato
    + preserved lemon orzo 74
  smash burger flatbread 111
tomatoes, tinned: chicken
    parmy 18
  chilaquiles with egg + feta 76
  chilli con carne con rice 42
  lasagne 26
  meatball + mozzarella orzo 51
tortilla chips: chilli con carne
    con rice 42
  chipotle pulled chicken
    with avocado + tomato salsa
    + tortilla chips 89
tortillas: chilaquiles with egg
    + feta 76
  tuna tostadas with avocado,
    jalapeños + pickled ginger 141

yoghurt: chicken or paneer
    biryani 148
  kale, salmon + sweet potato
    salad with a creamy garlic
    dressing 114
  pork + pineapple flatbread 86
  spiced lamb + aubergine with
    pitta 174
  spiced lamb steak with
    coriander + date chutney 156
  see also coconut yoghurt

Acknowledgements

Writing a cookbook has always been my biggest dream, and I'm not sure I'll ever fully process what this means to me. This book has only ever been a book of joy, love and self-care for me, as much as I hope it is for you, and that's all thanks to the incredible people around me. I can't believe my luck, and I couldn't be more grateful.

Firstly, to Marina De Pass and Ben Clark, thank you for working with me from so early on in this journey. I have no doubt that I would not be writing this right now if it weren't for your guidance, friendship, support and advice, and your care for me and for this book. Long may this team continue.

Thank you to my incredible editor, Celia Palazzo. I really hit the jackpot here. Thank you for sharing my vision and for always treating it with enthusiasm, respect and compassion. Thank you for your friendship and support along the way. This book is everything I could have wanted it to be and so much of that is because of you.

Thank you to Dan Jones, Saskia Sidey, Susanna Unsworth, Katherine O'Dwyer and Lauren Miller for making every photograph so beautiful and for capturing the feel of this book perfectly. Also, a huge thank you for making the shoot so welcoming and so much fun, and for hand modelling when I failed miserably.

To the entire Ebury team, especially Alice King, Lara Mcleod and Francesca Thomson, thank you for being the greatest, for having big goals for this book and working so hard to achieve them, and for always making it fun! Also, to Lucy Sykes-Thompson at Studio Polka, thank you for designing the book so beautifully and making our vision come to life. I can't believe I get to hold this book forever!

To my flatmates, Lara and Sophie, thank you for embracing the chaos that came with writing a book as soon as I moved in. Thank you for giving up your fridge space, for eating so many variations of recipes, and for your suggestions and support. Hearing 'mmm that is very enjoyable' (Sophie) and 'oh my god yum' (Lara) everyday was all the encouragement I could have needed. You're both a dream.

To all my friends, old and new, for your endless support. To have people like you in my life, who have never failed to encourage and share my work, from the very start, has made every part of this so easy. I love you and I'm so grateful to know you.

To my family, and particularly to my mum, Bridge, my sister, Anna, and my brother, Henry. You are the best. I couldn't have quit my job, followed my passions or written this book without you. Thank you for everything, thank you for always being there, and thank you for being my best friends. I love you with a great, big, ginormous love.

To my dad. Your sense of adventure, love for travel, and your humour and quick wit have influenced me in every possible way. I know you would be as proud of me as I am of you, and I so wish you were here to see this.

Finally, thank you to you, for buying this book. Thank you for sharing your stories with me, as I share my food with you. I thought about you every step of the way while making this book, and I hope you love these recipes as much as I do.

5

Ebury Press, an imprint of Ebury Publishing
Penguin Random House UK
One Embassy Gardens, 8 Viaduct Gardens
London SW11 7BW

Ebury Press is part of the Penguin Random House
group of companies whose addresses can be found at
global.penguinrandomhouse.com

Text © Eleanor Wilkinson 2024
Photography © Dan Jones 2024

Eleanor Wilkinson has asserted her right to be identified as
the author of this Work in accordance with the Copyright,
Designs and Patents Act 1988

First published by Ebury Press in 2024
www.penguin.co.uk

A CIP catalogue record for this book is available
from the British Library

ISBN 978-1-52992-197-7

Commissioning editor: Celia Palazzo
Production controller: Lucy Harrison
Design: Studio Polka
Photographer: Dan Jones
Food stylist: Saskia Sidey
Prop stylist: Lauren Miller

Printed and bound in Germany by Mohn Media,
Mohndruck GmbH

Penguin Random House is committed to a
sustainable future for our business, our readers
and our planet. This book is made from Forest
Stewardship Council® certified paper.

The authorised representative in the EEA is
Penguin Random House Ireland, Morrison
Chambers, 32 Nassau Street, Dublin D02 YH68.